The Best
Women's Stage Monologues
of 1998

Other books by Jocelyn A. Beard

100 Men's Stage Monologues from the 1980s

100 Women's Stage Monologues from the 1980s

The Best Men's/Women's Stage Monologues of 1990

The Best Men's/Women's Stage Monologues of 1991

The Best Men's/Women's Stage Monologues of 1992

The Best Men's/Women's Stage Monologues of 1993

The Best Men's/Women's Stage Monologues of 1994

The Best Men's/Women's Stage Monologues of 1995

The Best Men's/Women's Stage Monologues of 1996

The Best Men's/Women's Stage Monologues of 1997

The Best Stage Scenes for Men from the 1980s

The Best Stage Scenes for Women from the 1980s

The Best Stage Scenes of 1992

The Best Stage Scenes of 1993

The Best Stage Scenes of 1994

The Best Stage Scenes of 1995

The Best Stage Scenes of 1996

The Best Stage Scenes of 1997

The Best Stage Scenes of 1998

Monologues from Classic Plays 468 B.C. to 1960 A.D.

Scenes from Classic Plays 468 B.C. to 1970 A.D.

100 Great Monologues from the Renaissance Theatre

100 Great Monologues from the Neo-Classical Theatre

100 Great Monologues from the 19th C. Romantic & Realistic Theatre

Smith and Kraus *Books For Actors*
THE MONOLOGUE SERIES

The Best Men's / Women's Stage Monologues of 1997
The Best Men's / Women's Stage Monologues of 1996
The Best Men's / Women's Stage Monologues of 1995
The Best Men's / Women's Stage Monologues of 1994
The Best Men's / Women's Stage Monologues of 1993
The Best Men's / Women's Stage Monologues of 1992
The Best Men's / Women's Stage Monologues of 1991
The Best Men's / Women's Stage Monologues of 1990
One Hundred Men's / Women's Stage Monologues from the 1980s
2 Minutes and Under: Character Monologues for Actors
Street Talk: Character Monologues for Actors
Uptown: Character Monologues for Actors
Ice Babies in Oz: Character Monologues for Actors
Monologues from Contemporary Literature: Volume I
Monologues from Classic Plays
100 Great Monologues from the Renaissance Theatre
100 Great Monologues from the Neo-Classical Theatre
100 Great Monologues from the 19th C. Romantic and Realistic Theatres
A Brave and Violent Theatre: 20th C. Irish Monologues, Scenes & Hist. Context
Kiss and Tell: Restoration Monologues, Scenes and Historical Context
The Great Monologues from the Humana Festival
The Great Monologues from the EST Marathon
The Great Monologues from the Women's Project
The Great Monologues from the Mark Taper Forum

YOUNG ACTOR SERIES

Great Scenes and Monologues for Children
Great Monologues for Young Actors
Multicultural Monologues for Young Actors

SCENE STUDY SERIES

Scenes From Classic Plays 468 B.C. to 1960 A.D.
The Best Stage Scenes of 1998
The Best Stage Scenes of 1997
The Best Stage Scenes of 1996
The Best Stage Scenes of 1995
The Best Stage Scenes of 1994
The Best Stage Scenes of 1993
The Best Stage Scenes of 1992
The Best Stage Scenes for Men / Women from the 1980s

If you require prepublication information about upcoming Smith and Kraus books, you may receive our semiannual catalogue, free of charge, by sending your name and address to *Smith and Kraus Catalogue, 4 Lower Mill Road, North Stratford, NH 03590. Or call us at (800) 895-4331, fax (603) 922-3348.*

The Best
Women's Stage Monologues
of 1998

edited by Jocelyn A. Beard

The Monologue Audition Series

SK
A Smith and Kraus Book

Published by Smith and Kraus, Inc.
One Main Street, Lyme, NH 03768

Copyright © 1999 by Smith and Kraus, Inc.
All rights reserved
Manufactured in the United States of America

First Edition: September 1999
10 9 8 7 6 5 4 3 2 1

The Monologue Audition Series ISSN 1067-134X

NOTE: These monologues are intended to be used for audition and class study; permission is not required to use the material for those purposes. However, if there is a paid performance of any of the monologues included in this book, please refer to the permissions acknowledgment pages to locate the source who can grant permission for public performance.

Contents

Preface

I feel like a certain white rabbit. This book is late. To all of you actresses and theatrefiles I apologize. Thanks to the internet, I have more material than ever from which to choose and that can only be a good thing.

1998 was a solid season. Inside you will find exemplary examples of stage writing that will hopefully provide you with that perfect monologue.

Actresses looking for monologues with contemporary zing should check out *Dating Dummies, Swing Lab, Give Me Shelter, Mad Maenads (Wives),* and *Plastic.*

Those seeking more lyrical fare should consider *The Little Oasis, Islands of Repair, Something Is Wrong, Fantasyland,* and *Far East.*

Mature actresses will find stuff they can sink their teeth into in *Tidworth, Journey, The Interview* and *'Til the Rapture Comes.*

Comedic performers will find some giggles in *Wanda Dresses for the Evening; Alice and Rico; Full Moon, Saturday Night; Impossible Marriage; Monica,* and *Our Lady of Perrysburg.*

Good old-fashioned drama abounds in *The Resurrection Play, Singing in the Wilderness, Agamemnon, Evil Legacy, At the Inland Sea, The Crustacean Waltz,* and *The Inconvenience of Death and Friendship.*

Young performers will find some tasty tidbits in *Grace Notes, The Gift, Guanabana, Killer Joe,* and *Virtual Rendezvous.*

There's something for everyone in this book and as always, should you find something you like, READ THE PLAY!

I've gotta run. If I don't crank out the 1999 books, Marisa and Eric will kill me! Break a Leg!

Jocelyn Beard
The Brickhouse
Patterson, N.Y.
Summer 1999

This book is dedicated to Heather McNeil.
Yale blew it. Big time.

Agamemnon

Andrew C. Ordover

From the Atreides Plays of Aeschylus and Euripides

Scene: the palace of Agamemnon and Clytemnestra

Dramatic
Clytemnestra: murderous queen. 30–40

> *Vengeful Clytemnestra has just murdered her husband,*
> *Agamemnon and Cassandra, the seer. Here, she describes*
> *her dark deed.*

CLYTEMNESTRA: Behold your king. The conqueror.
   [*(The teacher sinks back to his knees. Orestes cries out and*
   backs away.)]
CLYTEMNESTRA: Much have I said before to serve necessity
But I will feel no shame
Unsaying all of it right now
Believe me, this is no new thing
But ancient bitterness
And pondered deep in time

I stand here as I stood there
When I struck him dead
The thing is done
I won't deny it now

So that he could not beat aside
His death
I caught him in his child's bloody clothes
As fishermen net their prey
I struck him twice
He floundered in his bath
He tried to rise

1

But on the second blow
He buckled at the knees and fell
When he was down I struck again
And thanked the gods for strength

Thus he went down
Life struggled out of him
And as he died, he spattered me
With dark red, violent driven rain
His bitter savored blood
To make me glad
Yes, glad
As flowers in rain

These being the facts
Be glad or be sorry
As you will
For me, I glory
No man deserved this fate more than he

He filled our cups with evil things Unspeakable
And now himself come home
Has drunk it to the dregs
    (She throws down the axe.)

That man is Agamemnon, my husband. He is dead, the work of
this right hand. I struck in strength and righteousness. And that
is that.

Agamemnon

Andrew C. Ordover

From the Atreides Plays of Aeschylus and Euripides

Scene: the palace of Agamemnon and Clytemnestra

Dramatic
Clytemnestra: murderous queen. 30–40

> *When she is struck down by her son, Orestes, Clytemnestra's*
> *wrathful spirit cries out for blood.*

CLYTEMNESTRA: Enough, you say?
You would go home and sleep?
And what use are you, if you sleep?

Look at these gashes in my heart
Think where they came from
I was slaughtered
Long before I died
And you were there

You think that you're immune
From all my hate?
You're not

Your race is mine
I know your names
I'm calling on you now
To be my Furies
Angels of Revenge
Go find the child
Hunt him
Kill him
Answer for my blood

Go seek Orestes
Look
You'll find him
With your secrets
Buried in this butchered world
Wherever you've been wounded
Wronged
You know where

If you don't
Beware, my friends
Your secret stores of
Cancerous hate
Are rising
Bursting
Even as we speak

You gloomy children of the night
This world is chiselled into you

Like stone
Like tablets you record it all
And teach it to your children

So don't act shocked
Or civilized
When I claim kinship to you

Take the axe
And find my boy
Go feel the joy of blood
Between your fingers
You've been aching for some
Justice
Honestly

You know you have
For years

Indulge yourselves
O audience of evil things
Pay off your debts
And make your country scream

The ghost of Clytemnestra
Calls your name

Alice and Rico

Jeff Goode

Scene: an interrogation room

Serio-Comic
Alice: a public defender. 30s

> *Here, a petty criminal gets a surprise when his attorney has what can best be described as a "moment."*

ALICE: Can I tell you something?

[RICO: *(Not sure that's such a good idea.)* Um—]

ALICE: I think I misjudged you. I'm sorry. The kind of client I usually get here…are real scum. Career criminals. Nasty swaggering assholes with no respect for anyone. And the only thing worse than their attitude, is their attitude toward women. You walk in here and the way they look at you, you know exactly what they want… And you know they can't have it. There's something really satisfying about having that kind of power over that kind of a man.

But you know what's even more satisfying?

The idea of throwing all that away. Stripping off the briefcases and bike chains and the roles we play and just becoming two naked primal forces throbbing and sweating together right here in front of everybody. Did you know that's a two-way mirror? I used to fantasize about it all the time.

But after you've done it a couple times, the idea really loses its appeal.

At the Inland Sea

Edward Bond

Scene: a young boy's fantasy

Dramatic
Woman: a young mother facing the murder of her child by the Nazis. 20–30

> *Here, dark images of the Holocaust come alive in the mind of a young boy who is homesick.*

WOMAN: I used to tell you stories. You were too little to understand. You knew my voice. You were so quiet. So still. I loved you even more then—I can never show my gratitude. *(Rehearsing.)* I'll carry heavy things. Fetch the shopping. You'll have my baby as hostage: I'll have to work. I'll live off scraps and snatch a half-hour's sleep in a corner with my baby... *(Half singsong.)* The world's a stone. The world's a stone. What can I do? I can't look at my baby. I can't look at the sky. I can't look at the end of the street. The lorries will come round the corner. If I told the soldiers a story. The right story. They'd listen like you did. They'd be still like you were. They couldn't kill you. All the soldiers sitting round me on the ground with their rifles. I'd hold you in my lap and tell the story. What story?...Tell me a story my precious. You know stories. That's why you were so still. Tell me a story—and you'll live. They'll hurt you, precious. You'll whine. *(Imitates a baby.)* "It hurts, it hurts"...It can't speak. *(Picks up a stone and asks it.)* Tell me a story! Tell me a story! Their uniforms are your color. Tell me the story. The world's a stone, the world's a stone! The things you've seen—you must know the story! It's crying! The stone! Crying! No! My tears! I cried! My tears fell on it... *(Drops stone.)* My baby's going to die. *(To the baby.)* I'll look at you when you're dead. They'll throw you on the heap of dead babies. I'll climb on the heap and look at all the faces. How will I know it's you? All

7

their faces are the same when they're killed. I'll know your hands. The hands will be the same! How will I know? *(Looks round, half calls.)* Tell me a story! I'll pay! *(Looks for something to pay with, feels inside the bundle.)* Look!—dirt from my baby's face! I'll pay you with that! Look how fine and soft and black! You could put it in a ring. When you went to heaven you could show it—they'd cry and let you in. *(Looks up.)* And all the sky—when it's black— is that dirt from the faces of dying babies? *(Picks dirt from the ground.)* Look! Dirt—to pay for the story! My baby was carried over that dirt! Take it! It's worth the story! Don't let them kill my baby!

The Beach Club

Ludmilla Bollow

Scene: a beach, December 1

Dramatic
Allegra: a young woman on the verge of suicide. 17–19

> *Allegra has returned to the beach, where her baby Jonathon was drowned, with the intention of killing herself. Here, she relives the boy's death one final time.*

ALLEGRA: *(In gentle scolding tones.)* I've told you to keep away from the water. You must stay near mommy. Always! *(Happier mood.)* Come, let's build another sand castle—away from the water. We'll build it together. Okay? *(Kneels in sand stage left, begins building imaginary sand castle. Laughing and giggling in process.)* Look how big it's getting, Jonathon. Let's build the biggest castle we've ever built. And, we won't knock this one down. We'll save it for Brady to see. Okay? Look Jonathon! How it glistens in the sunlight. Like millions of tiny diamonds piled one atop another. Castle's almost taller than you, Jonathon. *(Stops. Looks out.)* Look! There's Brady! *(Stands up.)* Brady's come to visit us. Maybe he'll help us build our castle. He's smiling, Jonathon— he's walking toward us. Now, he's laughing. Let's call to him. Come on, "Brady!" *(Laughs joyously. Pause.)* He doesn't hear us. Let's call louder—Brady!! *(Almost screaming.)* Brady!! He's turning away. He's leaving. *(Calls out frantically.)* Brady! Here we are! Over here! By the sand castle!…He's disappearing— *(Kicks at castle. Punches it down fiercely.)* He probably couldn't see us behind this castle. Stupid castle!

(Space Odyssey music begins. She looks about frightened.)
ALLEGRA: The other people—they're leaving too. They're all going away. And the sun—it's getting dark again. *(Lights dim somewhat. Calling frantically.)* You don't have to leave—just because

9

the sun's fading. You don't have to disappear too! *(Looks about wildly, then calls out.)* Jonathon! Where did you go? Come back, Jonathon! Don't go near the water—there's a big wave coming. *(Screams hysterically.)* Jonathon! Jonathon!!! *(Complete silence.)*

　　[JAKE: What's the matter, Allegra?]

ALLEGRA: *(Terrified agonized cry.)* Jonathon! *(Softly.)* Jonathon—he's gone…

Blue Yonder, "Spare Parts"

Kate Aspengren

Scene: here and now

Serio-Comic
Christine: a young woman with an unusual sense of family loyalty. 20s

> *Christine's body has been sued for surgical spare parts by infirm members of her family since she was a baby. Here, she speaks of her experiences and sense of obligation.*

> *(Christine is dressed in a gray sweatshirt and jeans. She is barefoot. She looks very tired.)*

CHRISTINE: When I was born, my family called me the miracle baby and my picture was in the *New York Times.* I guess you could say that I was famous. See, my big sister, Lisa, was sick. Dying. With leukemia. The only thing that would save her was a bone marrow transplant but they needed an exact donor. The closest donors are brothers and sisters. Did you know that? Lots of people don't know that. So when I was about a year old they took my bone marrow from *(Points.)* right here, in my hip you can still see the little mark and gave it to Lisa and she got well. Now she's married and has a little baby and a real nice house. I was even her maid of honor.

A lot of people got mad at my parents. They wrote nasty letters to the newspapers and called up the TV stations. Said my mom and dad only had me to save Lisa's life. That it wasn't fair because I couldn't give my approval for them to take out my bone marrow. But she's my sister, you know? Of course I'd want her to live. Besides, I don't even remember it so it couldn't have hurt that much, could it? I mean, if something hurts you that bad, wouldn't you remember it?

When I was about fifteen, my grandpa needed a new kidney.

His just weren't working right and they said he was poisoning himself from the inside. So I gave him one of mine. You only need one kidney anyway. Did you know that? You only need one kidney but you can't spare any grandparents, that's what my family said.

Then last year my dad got sick. He had something wrong with his lungs. I forget what it's called exactly but it was pretty bad. So they asked me would I mind, you know, giving up part of my lung for my Dad, and I said no, I wouldn't mind. Not for my Dad. Of course, I wouldn't mind. Got a big scar from that one goes from here clear over to here *(Runs finger from middle of chest to middle of back.)* and sometimes I still can't sleep very well from the nerve spasms I get. He ended up dying anyway.

There was some other stuff too. Skin graft for my cousin, a teeny slice off the top of my liver for my sister's little baby. Couple of inches of vein from my leg for my grandma.

People don't understand why I do it. But it's my family, you know. If they need a little piece of me to keep them going, I'll give it to them. I can't tell them no if they're counting on me. Can I?

Sometimes in my room at night I take off my clothes and look at myself in the mirror on the back of the door. I touch all the scars. Take an inventory of my parts. I don't know what will be next; it's hard to say.

I think maybe this is my calling, you know. We're taught that everyone is here for a purpose and I think this must be mine. I mean, it has to be.

Because when I was born, my family called me the miracle baby and my picture was in the *New York Times*.

Cornelia

Mark V. Olsen

Scene: Alabama

Serio-Comic
Cornelia: recently divorced member of a politically connected family soon to marry Governor George Wallace. 20s–30s

> *Here, Cornelia tells her mother she thinks the mercurial Wallace is about to pop the question and then some.*

CORNELIA: Thanks. Guess who's just about to pop the question.

[RUBY: Says who?]

CORNELIA: I got spies out the wazoo. He went to Silverman's yesterday to price a ring. A Wallace and a Folsom. George and Cornelia. Anthony and Cleopatra. It's so, so right. We're both supremely public creatures. We both photograph well.

[RUBY: They say there are deeper reasons for matrimony.]

CORNELIA: Don't think I haven't been laying in bed all morning thinking about that. I like sex, Mama. I'm just realizin' that. I've always liked flirtin'—but I like sex, too. I like it alot.

[RUBY: *(Growling, disgusted.)* I do, too, but it's 10:30 in the morning.]

CORNELIA: You ever look at his hands? Thick. The hands of a prize-fighter. He holds a fork—like a pitchfork, jabbing at the chopped steak—mmmmmmmm. Gives me gooseflesh. He's very strong. And a little mean. In a nice way. Not ugly mean. I mean just the kind of mean I like. All I know, I could stay in bed with him behind those green velvet curtains a zillion years. 'Til all the stars and satellites fall from heaven. When we're in that room—Oh God, Mama!—George, naked, dark skin and chest hairs and thick paws bending over me, draped on top of me—

[RUBY: Uughk, Cornelia—]

CORNELIA: Each time it feels like a million billion years when we're together. Like all eternity, from Adam and Eve straight through to the Second Coming— *(Giggles, then sets up her mother.)* And when I look at my watch? I can barely believe it only took four minutes.

[RUBY: Cornelia!]

CORNELIA: When we were together last night—"together"—I couldn't tell if I was dreaming or not. I couldn't tell what was me and what was him. A complete unity of souls. He's huffin' and puffin' away, his eyes spinnin' and dialatin'—it's very spiritual and religious. Know what else? He yanks my hair. He takes a handful and he yanks me to the left, then he yanks me to the right, and I'm squeelin' with delight—What do you think about that?

Cornelia

Mark V. Olsen

Scene: Alabama

Dramatic
Cornelia: recently divorced member of a politically connected family soon to marry Governor George Wallace. 20s–30s

> *The Wallace's marriage suffers greatly following the shooting that nearly took his life. When she discovers that George is engaging in phone sex, Cornelia taps his phone line. Wallace has discovered the tap and is furious. Here, desperate Cornelia tries to explain her fear and jealousy.*

CORNELIA: *(With deep fragility and honesty.)* Sometimes? I'm layin' next to you at night. And I'm so angry and resentful. At you. Then I float up to the ceiling and look down and all I see's two people layin' back to back, just staring off in opposite directions in the dark. And sometimes? When I'm on the road? Oh God I'm so glad to get outta here. Sometimes I can't get outta here fast enough. But I get confused cause even that first night, in some cold hotel room? I wanna come home. I put pillows where you ought to be laying beside me. I don't shine alone— *(Pause.)* We used to sit out at night. When the whole world was just a big front porch. And laugh and dream how we'd take the world by storm. And we did. I just want the dream back. All I've ever wanted is the dream back. And— *(Fighting tears.)* —if you don't know that? If I don't show it, or if—sometimes I do stupid things? It's hard to show it without gettin' at the part that breaks my heart, too—

The Crustacean Waltz

R. Thompson Ritchie

Scene: an inn on an islet in the Chesapeake Bay

Dramatic
Nay: a woman terrified of the future. 47

> *Nay fears that she is going to die from the same disease that killed her sister. Here, she reveals her sense of impending doom.*

NAY: All I want is to get away somewhere and burrow in until I can forget.

[SETH: Forget what? Me?]

NAY: You, Harriet, everything the last seven years.—And it hasn't ended. Nothing has ended. It's just hanging out there waiting to tap me on the shoulder.—I get up every morning of my life and wonder what dress to put on, because if I put on something I really like, something that makes me look young and slim and really chic…that might be the day when I get the news.—When the results come back positive, and I'll never be able to look at that dress again.

[SETH: You have to stop thinking about this, Nay.]

NAY: You're not listening to me.—I'm so beyond thinking, I don't recognize myself.—I mean, how did this happen? I never broke a rule in my life, I never drove a mile over the speed limit, I never even tried to use a coupon after the expiration date. And what do I get for it? I'm forty-seven years old with the worst genetic history anybody could imagine and a family of four to support— by myself!

[SETH: So what do you want to do?]

NAY: I want some respite.

Dating Dummies or The Inevitable Extinction of the Homo Sapiens

Elizabeth Ruiz

Scene: Southern California, 1970s

Serio-Comic
Lisa: a naive young bride. 20s

> *In college, idealistic Lisa fell in love with Erwin, a "genius socialist filmmaker." When they move to California, things go sour. Here, Lisa demands that Erwin find a job.*

LISA: Erwin. Erwin. Talk to me, Erwin. Why won't you talk to me? Are you still mad at me 'cause that guy punched you in the eye at Penn Station? Erwin, that was two months ago! We're in California! This was your big dream. The West Coast! On the fringe, self-sufficiency! Remember? Erwin, I told you what happened. If you hadn't stopped to talk to those drug addicts, that guy wouldn't have followed me into the subway. He was a pig! He asked me if I was a dyke and said he was going to…do me on the escalator. Ughhh. So, I gave him the finger. What was I supposed to do? Okay, so maybe it wasn't the smartest thing to do, but I was nervous. I didn't think it would cause a riot! At least he didn't get the ghetto blaster! *(Rapidly.)* I kicked him in the crack of his butt with my pointy boots after he punched you in the eye, it's not like I just stood there! He probably couldn't sit down for like a week. What do you want me to do? *(Pause.)*

Erwin, you have to find a job. You survived orphanages, military school, drug rehab, working for your Mafia stepfather, jail! You're supposed to take the lead! I had a sheltered childhood. I don't know what I'm doing!… All you do is sit there and stare at the television set. It's broken! Haven't you noticed? I went job

17

hunting for a month and all you did was put me down. "Only losers work as cashiers. You're too clumsy to wait on tables. How can you be a sales person if you have no presence. You can't type fast enough"…nana, nana, nana na. Well, listen here Erwin—I got us this apartment. I found the car. I got a job! And they won't even let me buy a beer in this…fuckin' town!

The Dreamers

Christina Harley

Scene: Melody County, North Carolina, April 4, 1968. The day of the assassination of Reverend Martin Luther King.

Dramatic
Princess: a woman in love with the dream of Martin Luther King. 20s

Here, idealistic Princess speaks to the slain civil rights leader of her own love and dreams.

PRINCESS: For the first time there was some hope! I have a dream... I have a dream that someday you'll walk in that door. Take away all the pain. All the hurt. Take me away to all them places you be talkin' about. I got me some dreams too...

[LOLA: You are just too much like my daddy was! A fine minister. God sent you to lead us out of bondage and into the promised land! God bless you...God bless you!...]

PRINCESS: ...I named my first baby Yolanda Martina and my second baby Bernice Martina. Yolanda lives with Aunt Penny in New York because it was gettin' too hard havin' two kids and workin' every day. So I had to send her away. I know it must be stupid to you that I dream you was my man. But there ain't nothin' wrong with dreamin'. Sometimes all you got is a dream. When anybody asks me who the daddy is I just say Martin is the daddy. Then they ask me who Martin is, then I tell them it's none of they damn business. I ain't sure who they real daddies are. It don't matter, though, because there's you...

[OTIS: You livin' in a dreamworld.]

PRINCESS: Uncle Otis says I'm livin' in a dreamworld. Well I'd rather live in the dream than to know the truth. That I really ain't nobody. What you think I got keepin' me here? My lovin' husband? My pretty clothes? My future? Just my dream. Just my dream. And I'm wakin' up fast...

Erotic Scenes in a Cheap Motel Room

Michael Hemmingson

Scene: a cheap motel room

Serio-Comic
Lori: a woman whose marriage is faltering. 20s–30s

> *Lori has agreed to meet her husband in a motel to spice up their sex life. Here, she phones a radio talk show while she waits.*

LORI: Hello? Hi. Am I on? Turn my radio down? Okay. Okay, there. Listen. I was listening to your radio show, I don't know why, I was listening, and noticed a lot of people talking about aliens and UFOs. Yes. Yes. And I just wanted to tell you, I wanted to tell someone this, I've never told anyone this: I think I was abducted by aliens when I was a child. My brother and I always got scared when we'd see those big-headed aliens during the end credits for *Star Trek.* You know when the show was over. Anyway, I remember, several times, I remember being led out of my house by these alien-type people, big heads and eyes and long fingers, and next I was in some sort of underground base, and I was put on a table, and there were all sorts of tables with other people. It was a huge place. And all sorts of computers. And human men in military uniforms. I was told "Relax, it is all a part of the Secret School." They said, "Don't be afraid," and the funny thing is, I wasn't. When I think about it now—and let me tell you I try not to think much these days—I wonder why I wasn't afraid. I'm afraid now. I'm scared and years later, I was abducted again, and in some room I was taken to were two beautiful young girls—they were part human, and part alien; they had big eyes and wispy blonde hair. They called me "Mommy." The aliens told me these were my hybrid children, a race known as, I remember this, known as the Essassani. They called me "Mommy." I never wanted anyone in the world to call me Mommy. I never called my own mother Mommy. I called her by her name, Claire. She said, "I want you to call me Claire." Hello? Hello? *(Puts phone down.)* After I met the children, the next thing I remember is that I was standing naked in the backyard, looking at the sky, and there was this large, yellow-glowing disc, this ship, a UFO, in the sky, and it flew away, and I just watched it. Then Gary came out. He said, "Honey?" I didn't want him to call me honey. I wanted to say, "I hate it when people call me honey!" He looked scared. I asked him, "Did you see it?" He said, "See what?" He was scared because I was standing naked in the yard and it was dark and cold out. "Come inside, Lori," he said, and I did.

Erotic Scenes in a Cheap Motel Room

Michael Hemmingson

Scene: a cheap motel room

Dramatic
Tina: a woman betrayed by her lover. 20–40

> *When Shella confesses that she's pregnant, Tina is destroyed.*
> *Here, she sits alone in the motel room with a gun and muses*
> *about her ruined relationship.*

TINA: If you could just see your way clear to coming over here for a little while and spending a little time with me. I just want to look at you again and see you walk around with your naked bosoms and hear you hum to yourself. I never saw anyone whose bosoms looked better when she walked around and hummed to herself. You know the story as far as this goes. Number one: She had to stop walking. Number two: Going ahhhhhhhhhh and going eeeeeeeeeeehhhhh and so on and so forth is not what I mean when I mean hum. In this dream I keep having of her, she is not humming; in fact, she is screaming. It is a different kind of screaming than the screaming you would expect when you talk about screaming. It is not scary screaming. Or scared screaming. Well, she could be scared—what the man is doing to her in the dream should make her scared, *could* make her scared, because she really *isn't* scared—well she doesn't *look* scared. It looks like she likes it so much that nothing anyone ever did to her was as good as what was being done to her now. This is why she screams; this is why in the dream she screams. You should see it—his whatsit deep inside her unmentionable. He's got straps on it and rings on it and rubber bands and buckles and spangles and shiny metal buttons on it. It's the biggest whatsit I ever saw or knew existed. It's more like a tremendous dead filthy dirty yucky fish with dust all over it than an actual whatsit of a man. Plus these things on it make it gleam like there's something wet all over it and it seems to be held together by these rubber bands which have, like, spools of dust all over them, hanging off-like. You ever see the back of a refrigerator? You know how there is this type of dust on the back of it? That's what I mean. And that's what the whatsit of this man looks to me like in the dream. You'd think it'd come off from all the time and effort that it goes inside and outside of her unmentionable. But it doesn't. It just stays there. When it comes out again—when, when his whatsit comes out of her unmentionable again, the dust on it is still there: There are these spools and spools of it, plus the fact it's so wet-looking, and so hard- and tough-looking, like the sort of rubbery dust that grows off a fish. She, in the meantime, is screaming from it, and screaming each time it goes deep inside her unmentionable; even though it looks to you, while you're watching, it looks to you like: *How can it possibly do that?* It looks to you it can't even *possibly*—it's like you want to say: "Look out! Look out! Somebody's going to choke to death from this—it's going to get so high from going inside her that it's going to choke her to death!" She's not scared of this, like I said. In fact, no, it is not she who is scared, in fact *it's him!* He's scared! It looks like it's going to get out of hand, so he's scared, it's going to get out of his control, and pretty soon no one looking at it will believe it's a dream anymore. It gets bigger and bigger and pretty soon there won't be any room for it, no room in that room, no room in the world. It's a monster whatsit! But you know what the scariest part is? The scariest part is all of the sudden she stops screaming and she looks away. She just lies there looking away from him, looking at the wall, and she's not screaming, she's not humming, she's not going   AHHHHHHHHHHHHHHH!!!!   or   EEEEEE-HHHHHHHHHHHHHHHHHHHHH!!! but she just lies there looking at the wall with her long-eyelashed, blinking eyes. How could some-one, with something that large and strange way up her dirty unmentionable, just lie there like that? Her naked bosoms crushed against the sheets and I—me!—wishing that she would just hum like she used to hum. But in this dream, when I look at what she's looking at, I see that she's looking at a dog. Or a frog. Or a combination of both. There's this half-dog half-frog in the room watching them and now *she's* the one watching the dog-frog and *that,* that's the scariest thing of all. That *really* scares the shit out of me. It does.

Evil Legacy

Kathrine Bates and Ted Lange

Scene: 15th century Rome

Dramatic
Pantasilia: earthy, robust, and full of life. Ladies' maid to Lucrezia Borgia. 20–50

> *When her pregnant mistress is forced by her family to have her marriage annulled, Pantasilia offers the following practical advice.*

PANTASILIA: OH MY LADY, six months with a bambino is not such a terrible thing. Those men, they are not so smart. You could stand before that Council di Cardinales and make them believe that…uh…the earth spins round the sun!

So, what is a woman to a man? I ask you this. Yes to some we are things to play with, of course, but there have been women in history that have ruled men by their wit. Think you about…uh…this Helen of Troy. Armies fought for the, for the, como se dice, bellisima of that woman. Cleopatra, she ruled a country. You are no less than these. You are the daughter of il Papa! What better way than to show this strength than to stand in front of these men and swear that you still have your virginity. Many wives, oh yes, they have done the same on the wedding night. Think of this. We have a big secret and the man, oh, they are dying to find out what is the truth.

So you look at each man right here *(She points to her eye.)* and you swear on the biggest Bible in la basilica di Santo Pietro that you are still the virgin. You must not give a clue that this is not the truth…not a blinking the eye, or a crooked smile, or look like this or look like that…uh…uh…no…no…very straight… now. I know to tell a lie is, perhaps…uh like a sin.

But you too Madonna mia you have been a wife. Tell me then, how else can we survive?

What, those Cardinales...You think they are going to make the test? Oh ho ho. Would they dare to shove the hands under the dress to find out what is the truth? Oh ho ho, bambina mia, no more to be nervous. It will be a beautiful day, a day we can remember, the day we made foolish the holy men of Roma!

Evil Legacy

Kathrine Bates and Ted Lange

Scene: 15th century Rome

Dramatic
Lucrezia Borgia: unhappy daughter of the infamous Borgia clan.
20–30

> *Decadence, murder, and incest were dark hallmarks of the*
> *Borgia family. When Lucretia realizes that her name will one*
> *day be synonymous with the Borgia's evil legacy, she pleads*
> *her innocence to those who will sit in judgment in the distant*
> *future.*

LUCRETIA BORGIA: But what of me, Sophia, what do you
know?…Don't turn away from me, child. What is it? What have
you seen? Tell me!!

I–I do not understand…What are these words you are saying…Th—that Papa and Cesare will be forgotten…I…I…it is
all…caught in my throat…Lucrezia Borgia will be the most reviled
woman in all of history???!!! A murderess! An incestuous
whore!? No! No! It cannot be! What is this? What does it mean?
I am not the sinner…it is I who was sinned against! Will they not
know this?

Papa, Papa, no, help me, help me! Dear God, will the forces
of hell ever release their hold on me?!?

The murders, the decadence, the incest…they will say I
invited it? Invited it! Madonna Del Cielo…The murders, no, no,
they had nothing to do with me…never…it was them…what?
They will say this ring held the poison? But it was Cesare's! I only
wear it now in memory of him???!!!! Ah, Dios no! *(She takes it
off.)* Take it! Take it away…give it to the dogs for all I care! I never
want to look upon it again!

The base entertainments of the Vatican…they will say I was

27

a willing participant…Never, never was I…my Alfonso had just been murdered in our bed! Papa forced me…I-I was barely coherent; my mind was lost…

Papa, Papa, Cesare, what have you done????…What have you done to me?…

Ah, Cesare, Cesare, in one matter they will have guessed the truth…the rumors, whispers…no one ever knew for certain, not even Papa…They will believe it of Papa, too? They are wrong. For all the sins Papa committed in his life…never did he touch me in that way. In this, at least, he was innocent…but what does it matter now? What does anything matter…?

It began as innocent child's play, what did I know? I knew nothing!

Cesare and I were leaning over a table one day, I was laughing at some funny drawings. We were so close, I could feel his breath…a natural thing, it was often that way…I noticed his breathing was becoming stronger, coarser; I felt him looking at me, he was moving toward me; he put his lips to my neck and pulled me close…I was so stupid and ignorant…As he took me in his arms, I felt his power and lost my own. I grew weak. We touched lips. It scared me, I tried to get away, but he held me against him…so tight, fiercely tight…I couldn't move…didn't want to move…my body…I was feeling things. Then he became gentle. I could feel my heart racing. Softly he parted my lips with his tongue…I did the same to him. The sensation was…indescribable. I wanted to please him, to do all that he desired. Cool, wet, strange sensations flooded over my body. I could hear my heartbeat…it was so loud. In a throaty whisper, he said to me: "I will be the first, Lucrezia…it is my place to teach you. Promise me I will always be first in your heart, promise me."

He was so strong…through my tears, I promised him…I felt my own passion rising inside of me and I-I lost control, I could do nothing but give in…yes, he took me and made me his own— and he never let me go.

How quickly my innocent world became one of power and fear and pleasure and pain…And somehow I survived it all! Yes, there were nights when I longed to shut my door to him, but there were other nights when I yearned for him to come to me... and I do not blame myself for it anymore! I lived with a punishing guilt that I would not wish on any living soul and by God that was enough! Only later did I come to understand that choice had been taken from me...in virtually all things, and I found a way to forgive myself for what had gone on before...but I am telling you now, with everything I am or ever hope to be...I curse the universe for this picture of the wanton villainess, the evil seductress, the murderous harlot. I was never that! I swear, I was never that! I deserve better.

My death, Sophia. When?...Some years away. Then, there is time enough. I must change this...this horrid legacy...I will do it...

How will I die? In performing my duty...childbirth? I have seen it myself...and I know what my last thoughts on earth will be. In my mind's eye, it will be Alfonso, I see, his blue eyes sparkling. We live in a simple village with gentle rolling hills all around; we are together, smiling, delighting in our little son as he runs and plays in the sun-drenched meadow... *(She kneels in prayer.)*

Dios mio, hear my prayer, for my heart is breaking in what I have learned this day. Forgive my transgressions, dear Lord. I-I know I have not lived as purely as you would have desired, and in penance I vow to live the remaining days in service to the poor and the sick, and I will be just and fair in matters of government, and I will win the respect of the people and I-I...

Oh, please dear God and all the saints of heaven, I beg of you, do not let the sins of my family damn my name for all eternity! Guide me in ways to change this. If I did not believe I could, it would be more than I could bear. Hear me, oh Lord, I beg of you! Hear me!

The Family Tree

Karen Smith Vastola

Scene: here and now

Serio-Comic
Elizabeth: a cancer survivor with unique insight. 30–40

Cancer has taught Elizabeth to prepare for the future. Here, she explains why she's become a Methodist.

ELIZABETH: Do you know I've recently changed religions? I mean, I've become a member of another faith, so to speak. Do you find that interesting? I find it amazing. Or at least, found it amazing. Now, I think nothing of it. As if I were always a Methodist. Born a Methodist. Not the Roman Catholic that I was baptized when I was six weeks old. My mother. God. My mother was horrified. Horrified. When I broke the news, about being a Methodist. Although there's not much to become. You just show up at the church on Sundays, sing some John Wesley hymns, and join your fellow parishioners for coffee and cookies after the service. Anyway, I told my mother on New Year's Eve. It had become a particularly boring moment in the festivities, the family party we have every New Year's. It was about ten-thirty. Everyone was laying all over the chairs and sofas in my sister's living room after having eaten and drunk too much. All except me, I hadn't drunk a thing. Methodists don't drink. That seemed to be another good reason to be a Methodist. There must be a lot of alcoholics in the Methodist church. Or recovering alcoholics. I was one. I hadn't had a drink in five years. I quit for health reasons. What a joke. So this was my fifth year of sobriety at the family New Year's party. And you know how those things go. You could always use a good buzz on to get through those things. So I was sitting there thinking about that fact and I tried to think of something I could say to liven things up. You know something I would probably say if I did have a good buzz on. I mean here we are, an hour and a half to ball-drop time. No one's talking. Everyone's just laying there staring at the twentieth century fireplace—the television. Only during the holidays it's not even television, if there is a child under twenty around or an adult male—it's Nintendo! We're all staring at the James Bond Golden-Eye Game. You know *(Hum theme music.)* daada dadad dada. My nephew has worked his way up from pistol to flame thrower to a.k.70. And I think, why not now? Why not drop the news right now. They can't be really angry with me for turning my back on eighteen years of Catholic education. They'll be grateful to throw some insults my way. They should thank me for relieving the boredom. So I say, nice and loud, to wake up the ones that are sleeping with their eyes open. "You know Janey and I have been going to the Methodist church for the past couple months." "What?" my mother says. That got her. She was just about to nod off into REM sleep, but that statement brought her back. "Now, Elizabeth, don't tell me you're going to a Methodist church. Roaring Methodist? And you're bringing your daughter? Now don't tell me you're doing that?" We've been doing it and we both enjoy it. Janey has found a little friend to play with in Sunday school and I like the desserts. "She likes the desserts," my sister screams and almost falls off her chair with laughter. "It worked," I say to myself. Two of them are up and breathing. So I send off another zinger. "I even baked some muffins and poured the coffee myself last Sunday." Well they all carried on for about a half hour with that news. My mother leading the pack with warnings about how once you do a coffee, little by little they'll sucker you into all kind of activities and before you know it you'll be washing the floors and then sleeping on them because they'll ask you for money and you'll give it all to them and then you'll have no place to live. Like Catholics never ask you for a dime, I could have countered. But I don't say much, just let them rave on. At eleven they run out of juice, but its got their adrenaline flowing again and several of them get up and walk around looking for even more to eat and drink. I'm satisfied with the results. They've been introduced to the topic. Now when my mother calls me on Sunday she won't be shocked to hear I'm at church and that it's not the Catholic one. Let them think what they want, they don't have to know the other reasons I became a Methodist, not yet. Let Janey think she's found a new playmate and not that in some of those Sunday school lessons they'll be some discussions about life and death and the sweet hereafter. You know just in case she has to try and understand it and I won't be there to explain. Not that I'm going to die anytime soon. Of course I'm not. The doctors don't think so. It's just that I may die sooner than everyone else I know. Or I may not. Everyone else I know could step off a curb tomorrow and be hit by a truck. That's what the doctors tell me when I want to talk about numbers and probability of cure or re-occurrence. So I'm just warning everyone out there. Don't count on anything. It could happen to all of you tomorrow. Anyway, the church will just be one more thing for Janey that will be there for her if I'm not. And they're all very friendly there and she likes their cookies too. And they'll know her and they would have known me. And that's the other reason I joined the church, because it's small and friendly and they know me. And if the time ever comes. I mean if it comes sooner rather than later, they'll know me and my husband and family won't have to decide whether to slip some old, half-in-the-bag Catholic priest a fifty or a hundred as they try and sum up my life in five simple sentences so that someone I don't even know can stand there in front of a dead person he doesn't even know and repeat the five big occurrences or concerns of my life punctuated by, "God rest her soul," or "She's found her peace now." I really don't want to leave that way. I mean I want some kind of personal association, even if my minister only says, "I liked her cranberry muffins, or sometimes I'd look over at her while she was singing a hymn and I'd see tears in her eyes or she always shook my hand and said good morning and sometimes complimented my sermon and she meant it." And he would have known me, when I was alive and not just dead... But that's not something you can easily explain to your family or your mother on New Year's Eve. So let them think I became a Methodist because I like their cookies...I do like their cookies.

Fantasyland

Mary Lathrop

Scene: a bedroom

Serio-Comic
Daphne: a married woman with an active fantasy life. 30–40

As her husband slumbers peacefully next to her, Daphne lets her imagination run wild.

DAPHNE: So okay, it's late at night. Lochinvar has fallen asleep over one of those stupid engineering magazines he's always bringing to bed, with his reading light and bifocals still on, his mouth slack and open. I mean, when you're married to them, they're not always that attractive, so instead you're going to think about a sexy man. Right? Think about his sexy mouth, imagining his chest has just a little bit of hair, tight and curly, you know, just around the nipples, and then he runs his finger down your neck, just like that, and you see his mouth say "I want you." Brain sex. Mmmmm. "I want you." Right?

Only then Romeo here starts doing that awful snuff, snuff snoring, and you have to keep saying, "Bill, roll over, roll over, honey." Only Bill's not rolling tonight. So you give up and turn on *Nightline* where Ted Koppel is interviewing some boring body about some boring billion dollar debt for…You know, Ted Koppel has a kind of interesting laugh, not a laugh, a chuckle, actually.

And so I am…not in my bed with my husband. No. I'm in…a hotel suite. Yes. And I am here because…in the morning I'm making America's presentation to the U.N. about the billion dollar debt. And Ted's on his way over right this second to brief me. I go to my suitcase, just to unpack, and pull out—surprise!—an important negligee. Wait a second, wait, how did nine hundred dollars worth of handmade French silk get inside my bag? A surprise from Bill? But (a) Bill doesn't believe in surprises, and anyway, (b) he's not going to spend the nine hundred when the house needs a new roof next year. A note. "To my loving wife: It's breaking my heart that we're apart, and the children are physically ill with missing you, but don't think of us. We are so proud of your important work for our country. If only I could be there to slip off this nightie tonight. Tomorrow, knock 'em dead at the United Nations. Yours faithfully, Bill."

Start again. Bill and the kids are fine, and they're on the other side of the continent, I don't have to think about them, whereas I am in a hotel room in a glamorous east coast city, and I'm here because…just because. And I'm wearing…my sweats. A knock at the door—it's Ted Koppel, who it turns out, has a rather sexy chuckle, and he's here because—come on, keep it simple—because he sat next to me on the airplane and we, well, we just caught fire with each other. Huh, Ted Koppel sat next to me on the airplane…Ted Koppel would definitely sit in first class, I think, so that means I flew first class… How did I come up with a first class airplane ticket? Bill, my darling Bill insisted that I use up all his frequent flyer miles, so that my flight would be enjoyable. Enjoyable? I used up all his hard-earned miles on a transcontinental flirtation with Ted Koppel.

Argggh!… I'm staring into the face of Ted Koppel. I don't know anything else. Ted, he says to me, with that sexy chuckle, you know he has that sexy chuckle, "We have some unfinished business." "How did you find me, Ted?" No, forget that part, it's too complicated: taxi cabs, explanations… And you've got to set the scene, figure a way out of your clothing, choose a caterer.

I'm on the deck of a million dollar yacht somewhere in the Aegean. I'm drinking a champagne cocktail and sunning myself naked, no, uh—no, I'm wearing a long, gauzy caftan. Ted Koppel, whose chuckle is even sexier, no longer appears on *Nightline*. No, now he's a fabulously wealthy French shipping magnate, and he's younger now, too, maybe only thirty-five. Actually, he isn't Ted Koppel at all. No, he's Andy Garcia! Yes. Andy Garcia, his black hair is slicked back, real European, you know, he brought me here, but he hasn't touched me…yet. He's been reeling me in, really slow. This is a world-class seduction, and I am the poached pear.

Oh God, what am I going to make when Bill's folks come for dinner tomorrow night? I completely forgot they're coming, and I promised I'd cook dinner. Uhhh, grilled salmon, easy, new potatoes, a Caésar salad, okay, poached pears for dessert, and there's some cookies in the freezer…

Stop! Andy Garcia is waiting! And he's getting a little impatient, standing there on the prow of the big yacht. I race back from meal planning and resume my position on the bow. Andy Garcia smiles down at me as I recline, recline supine, on the sumptuous deck where soon we will consummate our smoldering desires, explore the turgid landscape of our raging passions, here on the deck of this magnificent yacht, alone and adrift on the blue Aegean Sea.

He wants me. Andy Garcia is hungry for ME. The hot sun is beating in the rhythm of my heart. Andy Garcia says, "Darling, I want it to be slow this time; I want it to be thorough." My caftan magically floats away in the warm Aegean breeze. Andy Garcia, he drinks in my body with his bedroom eyes, his sexy eyes, and he says, "Agh! What are these lines on your stomach? What is this—cottage cheese on your thighs?" And he leaps overboard and swims away…Bye, Andy. It's pretty hard to get it right.

Unlike with Bill. With Bill, it's actually pretty easy to get it just right. I mean, he's the one who put ice on my neck when I puked with morning sickness every day for months, both times, with both kids, who actually watched as they came out of my vagina, who still kisses my baby-chewed breasts, and tells me with a straight face and in all sincerity that I am so beautiful. Who says, and I quote, that he wants to fuck me when I'm ninety. Ninety.

So you carefully slide Bill's reading glasses off his nose, put them on the nightstand, take the stupid engineering magazine out of his sleeping hands, mark the page for him so he can read it some more tomorrow night, lean across him, turn off the lamp, tap him softly on the shoulder, tell him, "Bill, roll over; roll over, honey," and when he rolls, you spoon up against him in the dark, run your fingers through the hair on his chest, just a little, you know, just the way he likes, just around the nipple, and you whisper in his ear, "I want you. Wake up, I want you."

Far East

A. R. Gurney

Scene: the American Naval Base at Yokosuka, Japan. 1955

Dramatic
Julia: wife of the base commander, unhappy and restless. 30s

> *Here, Julia confronts a young lieutenant with her feelings for him.*

JULIA: Oh yes. I'm avoiding the fact that I'm attracted to you.

[SPARKY: Hey, Mrs. Anderson…]

JULIA: No, I am. I admit it. I'm attracted to you. Maybe it's because you remind me of all those sweet boys I used to kiss good night under the lights outside our dorm at Smith, before they drove back to New Haven or Williamstown. Or maybe you make me remember those other boys, in their fresh new uniforms, whom I met after work at P.J. Clarke's in New York, and whom I also kissed, kissed good night, before they went off to war.

[SPARKY: Mrs. Anderson…]

JULIA: I said *maybe,* Sparky. Because I don't know all the answers. I do know how it feels to keep everything bottled up inside till you think you're going to explode, and so you try frantically to throw your attention onto something else, your job maybe, or when that goes sour, another person. But it doesn't work, and soon you're making someone miserable, and yourself even more so. So you get up at night, and wander from room to room, thinking of the one you could really love, wondering where is he now, is he with his girl, and why is he with her when he could be with me, and all you want to do is see him occasionally, just occasionally see him, and touch him, and dance with him, maybe just dance with him, that was fun, wasn't it, the dancing, and… *(Pause.)* Oh dear… *(Pause.)* Oh God. Now I've done it now, haven't I? Now I've really spilled the beans.

A Flower or Something

Jolene Goldenthal

Scene: here and now

Serio-Comic
Mattie: a woman with a unique hobby. 20–30

> *When her boyfriend broke up with her, Mattie was inspired to embark upon an unusual quest as she here relates.*

MATTIE: I've got something everybody wants. I'm not kidding. You look at me and you go "What?" Which only shows you don't know beans. *(She waggles her fingers in an exaggerated gesture.)* There's nobody's got what I've got. Honest. I'm going into the book. I was just like anybody else. Honest. Then it happened. I got dumped. This guy I thought was so great. Answer to my prayers and all. Well, okay. I've been dumped before. But this time I get dumped one night and the next morning, the very next morning… Are you ready for this? The very next morning I get fired. *(Pause.)* Well. That was a bit much. I sat down and I thought about it. I had nothing but time, right? I came up with the idea that what I need is something to make me different. Like *outstanding.* No guy is going to dump me like I am Ms. Nobody. And no boss is going to fire me if I don't want to be fired. *(Raising her hand.)* So I think "What?" Miss America I'm not. So that's out. I figure maybe shave my head. But I don't know. I'm kind of attached to my hair. Get a motorcycle? Zoom around? Mucho bucks. Let that go. I keep on thinking and then it comes to me. *Nails. Really long nails.* Everybody wants them. It's a business f'Chrissake. Those dinky little plastic fakes. Paste them on, ruins your nails underneath. So that's when it came to me. *Really long nails.* All I had to do was wait. No cost. Nothing.

So I think like one hand. Let them grow on one hand, keep the other hand short. So I do it. And they grow like crazy. So by now I'm getting some attention. I've got people, strangers, asking me "How're the nails today?" And I begin to worry, you know. I mean I've been lucky. But still… Maybe I'm supposed to put some kind of cream on them or something. Maybe eat something special. Forget it. They grow. They grow so one of them curls itself around another one and another one and I tell you, it is some sight.

At night sometimes when I'm not doing anything, say maybe it's a tummy going ouch on the tube, or one of those headache things, I stretch out my hand. I hold it near the light and it looks like something. A flower or something. Or curly fries, maybe. I figure I'm ready for the book. Okay. A couple more inches maybe, and I'm really ready.

Somebody told me about some Chinese emperors way back. They let their nails grow really long to show they never had to work, or something. But, hey, I'm working every day. Oh, yeah. I got a new job. No problem. *(She laughs.)* There's this guy comes in where I work. He sits around, watching me. So this one day he's sitting and watching and he goes "What're y' trying for? Disability? Y' wanna be disabled? Sit home an' collect?"

I take a deep breath. I smile. He's a customer, after all. "It's only the one hand," I tell him nicely, like I don't give a care.

So this character goes, "It's a *hand*. Not a fuckin' *ornament!*" He shakes his head, sort of sad. "So what's it all about?" He goes, "What goes on upstairs?" *Well.* I feel like giving him a good slap in the face or something. But then I figure he's not worth it. Here I'm maybe ready for the book and I had my picture in the paper…

I think like this. What's Madonna got? Nerve. And Julia? that big smile. And me? I've got my nails. *(She holds up her hand, admiring, and slowly, very slowly, she exits.)*

Full Moon, Saturday Night

Amy Beth Arkaway

Scene: here and now

Serio-Comic
Psychic Chick: a young married woman obsessed with all things psychical. 20–30

> *Psychic Chick has phoned a crisis hotline seeking advice about her cross-dressing husband but ends up giving spiritual advice to the phone counselor.*

PSYCHIC CHICK: It's karma. I keep telling you. It's like the universe is always watching and keeping score so even when you think you're being good, it'll sneak up on you and give you a swift kick in the caboose with a pair of nine-inch spiked heels and a stun gun. No getting around it. It's just I didn't think it would catch up with me so fast.

I think it takes longer than that. It's like you accumulate good and bad points or something, you know? Like the stuff that's happening now is probably payback for something I did God knows, maybe three, four lifetimes ago. God only knows what poor sucker will have to do time over my bad stuff now. I mean I could be some little old man who owns an ice cream truck, minding my own business, giving away free Strawberry Shortcake pops to needy kids, and boom my truck will just explode right there in the middle of the street and I'll wind up in some old age home—not the nice kind, but the welfare kind where they eat food that resembles cat food and they only get regular TV and there's only one so everyone fights over *Wheel of Fortune* or *Golden Girls* reruns And I'll be sitting there, with Jell-O drool all over my state-issued drab green pajamas, wondering just what I ever did to deserve this. Of course, it may wind up that I gave away all those Strawberry Shortcakes to the poor kids because no one was buying them and I had to unload the inventory and it turns out the truck explosion was really the work of some vandals who subscribe to *Soldier of Fortune* or some other neo-nazi-type publication, who were basically fed up with not picking their own free flavors, in which case the next poor fool will have that on her karma and on and on we go until I get it right, which I'm beginning to think will never happen *(Exasperated.)* You're not paying attention again. It's not what I did now, it's what I did who knows when or what? Got that?

The Gift

Simon Fill

Scene: a concrete park in Manhattan

Dramatic
Jones: a girl whose boyfriend has committed suicide. 16

> *Life's fleeting nature is sadly illustrated by Jones' assessment*
> *of the relationship she had with a boy who took his own life.*

JONES: We'd only known each other, like, three weeks. And we'd just started like, you know, like, doing it. He was quiet. But he said he loved me. Then, you know, like, we started doing it more, he got more and more intense about it, and my whole body was…air. Every moment we had we'd be doing it. I loved him, he loved me. And I was…air. Then the air blew away. He was gone. *(Pause.)* I thought he was lovin' me more. I thought he was happy. That's why he wanted to so much. But he was usin' me to hold onto life. And the string broke with no sound. *(Silence.)* Like, I'm sorry. I oughta go.

[JOHN: Like, don't.]

JONES: Know what I wrote in my diary? "I walked on the edges of someone else's sadness." But I should've known something, don't you see? His laugh sounded to me just…like a laugh.

Give Me Shelter

Wendy Weiner

Scene: a woman's residency in the Union Square area of N.Y.C.

Serio-Comic
Katie: a pragmatic bride-to-be. 20s

> *Here, a graduate student on her way to married-couples housing welcomes the new girl.*

KATIE: Bags packed, key returned, post office notified. *(She looks up.)* Aaaagh! Hello. I didn't hear you knock. Oh, oh, oh, you're the girl who's moving in here. No, no, they did tell me, I just completely forgot. I have so much on my mind.

I'm getting married today. City Hall. I am so happy, so thrilled, so ecstatic, to be leaving this place. Why? Why? Shared showers, shared kitchen, no visitors, no phone, meals that are—indescribable. To sum, the entire experience has made me want to die.

What's your name? Diana! Oh, how exquisite. I've always wanted a name like that. Katie. Not even Katherine, which has some dignity. Katie. It signifies nothing. It refers to nothing. But Diana! Mmmm. No, really? You don't know where the name Diana comes from? You really should.

In Roman mythology, Diana was the virgin goddess of the hunt. She was a very solitary goddess, except for the animals which always surrounded her. Perhaps the most seminal story about Diana recounts an incident where she was bathing naked in a mountain stream, as she was wont to do. A young hunter, Acteaon, came upon her and she was just so extraordinary that he stood there watching. Diana looks up, sees him, and grows instantly enraged. She dips her hands into the water, showers him with a few drops, and he is instantly transformed into a deer. Ultimately, he is hunted down and killed by his own pack of hounds.

Sad? Hmm. I've always rather liked that ending. I mean, ontologically speaking, if I may, this story is merely an ancient example of the oppression of the male gaze. Actaeon is no different than the men on our city streets who feel entitled to yell out such epithets as "Hey, sugar mama," "Nice butt," "I'm just a baby, I want to suck your tittie." *(Pause.)* But, I digress. It's a lovely name.

Oh, so you're new to the city? Mm-hmm. Yes, you look it. Sort of that deer-caught-in-the-headlights look. Or that Actaeon-caught-at-the-pool look. *(Laughs at her own joke.)* Well, welcome! You're going to adore the city. Well, most of it. There are places you should not go. Hell's Kitchen, Alphabet City, Washington Heights. You never want to go too far east or too far west—or to any of the boroughs. Otherwise, you'll be fine.

Where are you from? You. Are. Joking. Really. God, I thought that was just a setting for Jim Jarmusch films. So, what's brought you here? Are you on some sort of budget vacation?

Oh, you're staying here while you look for an apartment? Hmm. No, no, no, I just hope you find a place soon. You know they don't let you stay for more than a month. Mmm-hmmm. It's a new rule. *(Laughs.)* But then, that's not my problem!

Oh, no, no ring. No, it's not quite like that. See, god, it's all happened so fast; this was just last week. Ron and I were sitting in Loeb Hmm? Oh, Loeb Student Center. I'm matriculating at N.Y.U. Ph.D., Mythopoetic Comparative Anthropology. *(Smugly.)* Thanks.

Anyway, we're sort of moaning about our lives. He's living in this nightmare dungeon over on Avenue B with god knows how many other people, and I'm—well, look around you, when we overhear this woman saying how she just got married and moved in with her husband to Married Student Housing. Well—here comes the bride!

Oh, no. I don't even know that he likes women, honestly. Who cares? I'm getting a room, a kitchen, a bathtub!

Well, I'd best be going. *(Looks around room.)* What can I say? Good luck.

Grace Notes

Rachel Rubin Ladutke

Scene: a farm house in Connecticut, 1967

Dramatic
Catherine: a young woman who has just given a baby up for adoption. 19

> *Catherine is haunted by nightmares following her pregnancy. Here, she turns to her younger sister, Emily, for help.*

CATHERINE: Christ, Emily, just shut up for once, huh?
(They smoke. Emily coughs a little.)
CATHERINE: Every time I get to sleep, I keep having the same dream. I'm walking through this long hallway, and there's nobody else around. Except, I'm walking a little dog. It's really friendly and it loves me. All of a sudden this door opens—I didn't even see it. It's at the end of the hall, right in front of me. There's a really bright light, and voices, and I start feeling faint. The next thing I know, I wake up and the dog is gone. Just when I open my eyes, I hear the door slam shut. As soon as I feel like I can get up, I turn the door knob, but it won't open. I try and try, but the door is locked tight.

I start crying and screaming, and then I see a window and I notice it's snowing out. So I go outside, and I start dancing in the snow. I feel so free, I can almost forget about losing the dog. Off in the distance I see a little building, and I start running toward it. When I get close enough, I see that it's an animal shelter, and I realize what I really want is to get another dog. But the woman in the shelter says I can't. Somehow she knows I felt happy when the dog disappeared, and she tells me I don't deserve another one. I beg and beg her, and finally she agrees to let me look at their dogs. But I can't find any like the one I lost, and that's the only one I want. I start crying. Then I wake up, and I'm really crying.

I don't remember much about giving birth, but I remember I heard her cry. I didn't get to look at her, or hold her. The nurse even said I didn't deserve to see her, because I was giving her away. They did let me feed her once. I had to refuse to sign the papers before they'd even let me do that. She had blue eyes. I think most babies have blue eyes, but hers weren't at all pale. They were really deep, deep blue. Like the ocean. One hour, that's all we had together. Then they took her away again.

You know what I really don't get, Emmy? When I talked to the other girls at the agency, they all kept saying they couldn't wait to give birth so they could get back to normal. But I didn't want to have the baby, because then I was going to lose her. I tried to keep her with me as long as I could. I started having pains in the middle of the night, but I didn't wake Mom up until I couldn't stand it any more. I didn't want to go to the hospital, 'cause I knew I'd be coming home alone and empty. That's the worst part, I think. I feel so empty. I'm cold all the time.

And now everyone expects me to just go on like nothing happened. They lied to me. Nobody told me it would be like this. I'm not even twenty years old, Emily, and I feel like my life is over. Or a part of my life, anyway. And I just keep waiting for it to stop hurting. But it doesn't. It just gets worse. You don't know how much it hurts.

[EMILY: I'm sorry.]

CATHERINE: Emmy. Hold me?

Guanábana

Elizabeth Ruiz

Scene: a village near Oriente, Cuba, 1958

Dramatic
Luz: a young clairvoyant woman. 18–20

> *Luz's clairvoyance is encouraged by her father but punished by her mother, who is convinced she will eventually go mad. Luz uses the guanábana fruit to focus her mind when she looks into the future. Here, she asks the guanábana to help her conquer her own fear of madness and desire.*

LUZ: *(Taking out a guanábana.)* He loves me, *(Taking out another.)* he loves me not, *(Another.)* he loves me, *(Another.)* he loves me not, *(Another.)* he loves me, *(Another.)* he loves me not, *(Removes the last one.)* he loves me! (She holds it reverently.) Oh, Guanábana. Lately I am tormented by thoughts that scare me. Thoughts that feel so right yet so wrong. Whenever I think them, which is most of the time, I get this terrible pain right here. *(She touches her chest.)* I feel like my heart is growing larger and larger, and stretching and swelling into the rest of my body. Pressing into my lungs until I can't breathe, pushing up into my brain until I'm dizzy with confusion, filling my stomach until I'm nauseous and terrified, and rubbing up against…other parts… And my entire body throbs and I break into cold sweats and tremble with fear and anticipation. I can't eat or sleep or anything. It's horrible, horrible. It's the worst feeling I've ever felt in my whole life. And the worst part is…I like it. Isn't that awful? Help me Guanábana. Help me or my mother will send me to have a lo…lo…lo bottom of me. It runs in my family, you know. The sickness. Have pity on me for I am a weak and pitiful girl.

Guanábana

Elizabeth Ruiz

Scene: a village near Oriente, Cuba, 1958

Dramatic
Luz: a young clairvoyant woman. 18–20

> *Luz has allowed her special talent to be exploited by one of
> the leaders of the people's revolution. His virtual prisoner, Luz
> teeters on the verge of madness. Here, she has a breakdown.*

LUZ: "Ay Mama Ines   "Hey Mama Ines
   Ay Mama Ines   Hey Mama Ines
Todos los negros tomamos cafe!
All of us negroes drink coffee!"
(Repeat.)
Ay Mama Ines
Ay Mama Ines
Todo los negros tomamos Cafe."
(With enormous theatrics.)
That's right Aunt Matilde, life is short and I want to LIVE it. Don't
call me Luz. I am no longer Luz Teresa Esperanza Garcia Cabellero.
I am Cuba! Cuba del Sol. My pictures are on every major billboard
in Havana. So what if I pose in teeny bikinis, shave my pubic hair
and am seen around town with show girls of questionable repute
and millionaires with semiprecious snot up their noses, I am still a
virgin. An independent woman yes, a celebrity yes, but a virgin.
A good Catholic girl. And I am going to show you what it is to be
a modern virgin! *(She shimmies and wiggles seductively.)* Good
evening ladies and germs, women and sperms, rich and poor,
strong and weak, murderers, saints, chocolate and vanilla, lily of
the valley so white and alabaster, even so, I am the master 'cause
white wrinkles faster and black don't crack, Mijita! *(She laughs
wildly.)* Fancy, down and dumpy, brilliant and stale ones, to the

unborn and the dying, welcome, welcome, to el show del Club Sierra. Let us jiggle and shake, rock and rumble, slide and tumble and clutch the wet earth with our nails when our feet give out under the frenzy of bullets con guaguancó. We will dance in defiance of all political alliance, so repeat what I say, every night, every day "If I can't dance, mi negro, I WANT NO PART OF THIS REVOLUTION, OLE! *(She bows dramatically as if a huge crowd applauded.)* Tonight's show will be a little bit different. No singing whales, no bald men with tails, no lady with three titties, no kids with hairy tongues…because READ MY LIPS…there will be no more sugar, no more coffee, no more rum! No more easy piece of tail, no Havana cigars, no limousines; dear sweet drag queens, hide your lipstick and rhinestone tiaras, 'cause there will be no pretty boys waiting to dance with you! And as you know, Damas y Caballeros there's never been a single lesbian in all of Cuba's history, only thousands of old maids with very short haircuts. There will be very few guanábanas and very little thinking. There will be only dead, lifeless faces, and bony fingers, and eyes receding with longing into the next world! And I don't mean Miami. But here's something: Parents will be forbidden by law to beat their children and certain ducks will grow up to be swans. Flowers will bloom, bees will make honey, and still die like drones under the queen bee's caresses. Dogs will still be loyal and sex will still transport us to the spirit world,…babies will still vomit on our shoulders, and give us their sweet toothless grins…and cry for mama's milk…

Children will cry for their mothers…children will cry for their mothers… *(Her performance breaks down.)* I…I didn't want to leave you Angel. But I was afraid. *(Crying.)* I was afraid I'd be like her. Afraid I couldn't love you.

[GABY: Luz…]

LUZ: I used to have insides, you know. I remember. I was whole. I had dreams and imaginary friends. I had angels who promised to watch over me forever, but as I grew older, everything I was and felt, left me. I could feel it, vanishing through the pores of my skin, in the drops of sweat falling down into the earth which is the only thing related to me in this whole world.

A cruel and brutal father I could understand. Many girls live through that. It prepares them for a future of men too angry or broken to love. But to have a heartless mother is the greatest cruelty of all. You see she was empty. She was empty and she emptied me. I don't know how exactly but she did it, see. See? Look.

The Handless Maiden

Jeremy Dobrish

Scene: here and now

Dramatic
Ann: a woman returning to her husband after a fling. 30s

> *Although Ann has enjoyed a recent dalliance, she here endeavors to make peace with her husband.*

ANN: I was standing there you know? Surrounded by a world of possibilities and the phone was ringing. And I closed my eyes and tried to imagine perfection. I could have anything I wanted. Any whim immediately fulfilled in my mind's eye. I blinked and was surrounded by my perfect pottery. Blinked again and was surrounded by my perfect poetry. But in every imaginable permutation of perfection, I kept seeing you standing there with me. The two of us as kids filled with hope. That's all I've ever wanted.

[DAVE: I love you.]

ANN: I love you. And I'm sorry I left you like that. That was hurtful and irresponsible, but it was something I had to do.

[DAVE: I know.]

ANN: I want the world to be open for us. And I need you to hear me.

How I Learned to Drive

Paula Vogel

Scene: here and now

Serio-Comic
Female Greek Chorus: a commentator. Any age.

> *Here, the chorus steps forward into the role of Mother as she recites "A Mother's Guide to Social Drinking."*

FEMALE GREEK CHORUS: *(As Mother.)* A mother's guide to social drinking:

A lady never gets sloppy—she may, however, get tipsy and a little gay.

Never drink on an empty stomach. Avail yourself of the bread basket and generous portions of butter. *Slather* the butter on your bread.

Sip your drink, slowly, let the beverage linger in your mouth—interspersed with interesting, fascinating conversation. Sip, never…slurp or gulp. Your glass should always be three-quarters full when his glass is empty.

Stay away from "ladies'" drinks: drinks like pink ladies, slow gin fizzes, gold cadillacs, Long Island iced teas, margaritas, piña coladas, mai tais, planters punch, white Russians, black Russians, red Russians, melon balls, blue balls, blue Hawaiians, green Arkansans, hummingbirds, hemorrhages and hurricanes. In short, avoid anything with sugar, or anything with an umbrella. Get your vitamin C from *fruit.* Don't order anything with Voodoo or Vixen in the title or sexual positions in the name like Dead Man Screw or the Missionary. *(She sort of titters.)*

Believe me, they are lethal.… I think you were conceived after one of those.

Drink, instead, like a man: straight up or on the rocks, with plenty of water in between.

Oh, yes. And never mix your drinks. Stay with one all night long, like the man you came in with: bourbon, gin, or tequila 'til dawn, damn the torpedoes, full speed ahead!

How I Learned to Drive

Paula Vogel

Scene: here and now

Serio-Comic
Female Greek Chorus: a commentator. Any age

> *Now as Aunt Mary, the chorus speaks about her complex relationship with her husband, Peck.*

FEMALE GREEK CHORUS: *(As Aunt Mary.)* My husband was such a good man—is. Is such a good man. Every night, he does the dishes. The second he comes home, he's taking out the garbage, or doing yard work, lifting the heavy things I can't. Everyone in the neighborhood borrows Peck—it's true—women with husbands of their own, men who just don't have Peck's abilities—there's always a knock on our door for a jump-start on cold mornings, when anyone needs a ride, or help shoveling the sidewalk—I look out, and there Peck is, without a coat, pitching in.

I know I'm lucky. The man works from dawn to dusk. And the overtime he does every year—my poor sister. She sits every Christmas when I come to dinner with a new stole, or diamonds, or with the tickets to Bermuda.

I know he has troubles. And we don't talk about them. I wonder, sometimes, what happened to him during the war. The men who fought World War II didn't have "rap sessions" to talk about their feelings. Men in his generation were expected to be quiet about it and get on with their lives. And sometimes I can feel him just fighting the trouble—whatever has burrowed deeper than the scar tissue—and we don't talk about it. I know he's having a bad spell because he comes looking for me in the house, and just hangs around me until it passes. And I keep my banter light—I discuss a new recipe, or sales, or gossip—because I think domesticity can be a balm for men when they're lost. We sit in the house and listen to the peace of the clock ticking in his well-ordered living room, until it passes. *(Sharply.)*

I'm not a fool. I know what's going on. I wish you could feel how hard Peck fights against it—he's swimming against the tide, and what he needs is to see me on the shore, believing in him, knowing he won't go under, he won't give up—

And I want to say this about my niece. She's a sly one, that one is. She knows exactly what she's doing; she's twisted Peck around her little finger and thinks it's all a big secret. Yet another one who's borrowing my husband until it doesn't suit her anymore.

Well. I'm counting the days until she goes away to school. And she manipulates someone else. And then he'll come back again, and sit in the kitchen while I bake, or beside me on the sofa when I sew in the evenings. I'm a very patient woman. But I'd like my husband back.

I am counting the days.

Impossible Marriage

Beth Henley

Scene: a country estate just outside Savannah, Georgia

Serio-Comic
Floral: pregnant, at the crossroads of a complex life. 30

> *Floral's younger sister, Pandora is about to marry Edvard, an older man. Disapproving Floral here confronts the groom on the morning of the wedding with a bit of petty ire.*

FLORAL: Last night there was a little misunderstanding between us that I must rectify. When I said there could be a circus performing under my skirt, I was implying—it was meant to be a joke. I was attempting to indicate, I was wearing a tent, a large, billowy dress. Because of the pregnancy I was so big and wearing such large garb, i.e., tents, that a circus could or would be capable of performing underneath. You (I assume) assumed I meant I could service a whole circus, I mean an entire company of clowns or whatever could come under my skirt with their lascivious little ladders and horns and party, party, party, or whatever. Actually, it was a joke I could have phrased more carefully. Still your interpretation was not warranted.

[EDVARD: In attempting to follow your amorphous train of thought, I seem to have derailed.]

FLORAL: In any case, I'd like you to know I'm extraordinarily particular about who I see privately. I'm not a virgin, but other than that, I am wholesome in the extreme. Having said that, I beg you to leave.

The Inconvenience of Death and Friendship

Lisa Haeber

Scene: here and now

Dramatic
Lillian: a woman trapped in a dead-end marriage. 30–50

> *Lillian can no longer communicate with her social and career-minded husband, Roger. Here, she does her best to spell out her misery.*

LILLIAN: Roger? Did you ever feel so miserable that you wanted to die? Not that you had enough energy to actually kill yourself. But that you just willed yourself not to be? But then you were afraid that even if you did kill yourself, you'd just wake up on the other side and be without a body but still be conscious. I mean, that's what suicides are trying to kill: their own consciousness. And if anything survives death, and I'm terrified it does, it must be consciousness. So the whole thing would have been for nothing. But it's all for nothing anyway. Because there's no pleasure left in anything anymore. Not eating or working or getting drunk or having sex. Did you ever think about how pointless it all is? I mean, even the guy who cures cancer. I mean, he'll cure that and people will start dying of something else. And he'll die too even though he was so smart as to be able to cure cancer. And given enough time, no one will even remember that he cured cancer, or his name, or that he ever was. People won't even remember cancer. They'll say, "What's cancer?" Did you ever think about that, Roger? Of course, reincarnation might solve that problem, in the sense that if you come back, you get to bring with you all you learned before, even if it is difficult to access that information. But if there's anything more depressing than thinking about death being the end, it's thinking about reincarnating and having to do it all over again. Don't you ever think about that, Roger?

The Interview

Faye Sholiton

Scene: The Beachwood, Ohio, home of Bracha Weissman, January 1995

Dramatic
Bracha: a Holocaust survivor. 69

> *Bracha has agreed to be interviewed about her experiences in the Holocaust for a myriad of complex reasons, not the least being to help repair her damaged relationship with her daughter. Following several failed efforts to give the interviewer more than biographical information, Bracha finally breaks down and begins her relentlessly horrifying narration, an act that will finally begin to cleanse and heal her troubled soul.*

BRACHA: You want to know about my sister?

[ANN: Later, Bracha. On tape.]

BRACHA: I killed her.

[ANN: Don't, Bracha.]

BRACHA: She was off working when the Germans came for the mothers and the children. I was in the cupboard hiding with the baby.

Shush! Gitteleh. Shhh! Shhh! She won't stop crying. They're kicking down the door and grabbing us and pulling us in the middle of the room. "I'm *not* the mother!" I scream at the top of my voice…

[ANN: Please…]

BRACHA: Then they take her from me. Right from my arms. When Rifka comes in, she sees my face and flies out to the platz where they're taking everybody. *(Beat.)* She's running after a dead baby. *(Beat.)* I never told her.

[ANN: Rifka died because she was a Jew, not 'cause she was your sister.]

BRACHA: And now let me tell you the story about how I killed my son.

[ANN: Stop it, Bracha!]

BRACHA: When I was carrying him, every day and night I pray to God to make him safe. I have the same nightmare over and over. I'm in the closet with him and he's crying like a puppy, not a human being. I can't make him stop.

Then, when he's born and he's whole, I want to hold him all the time. I won't let him whimper, even.

My Max and I are having terrible fights about it. *(To the candle.)* "You can't protect him," he tells me. "You teach him to take care of himself."

So I raise him to be big and strong. He wins all the awards at school and the state title in wrestling. Nobody tells him what to do.

...And he graduates from high school. Early yet. Gets accepted into three different colleges, with a scholarship. But in the middle of everything, he goes to Israel. Enlists in the Army.

Who knows Israel is going to go to war? And this beautiful boy, who never hurt anybody,...

[ANN: You didn't send him there.]

BRACHA: Sure I did! When Manny died, I realized something: Death follows me.

Islands of Repair

Leslie Bramm

Scene: a life raft in the middle of the ocean

Dramatic
Woman: marooned at sea with her husband. 40–50

> *Several days have passed with no sign of rescue. Here a ship-wrecked woman muses on the ravages being inflicted upon her body and the state of her marriage.*

WOMAN: My hair is a mess. A mess The wind, the sun, the salt… Look at my hands, my feet. The bottom water, the only water, the only way we've survived, has left quarter-sized welts all over my legs. Everytime they start to heal, the salt rips them back open. *(Beat.)* I have no smell. No smell that I might recognize. All that I smell is salt! Salt in my hair, my skin, peeling off my lips, clogging my pours… *(Beat.)* What's happening to my body?

(Lights shift subtly toward rain.)

WOMAN: There is something inside of me. There has to be. Some feeling left, some bit of life. *(She painfully peels off her shirt. Her shoulders and back are badly burned. She tries to cover the burns with a small tube of lip balm.)* I'm turning into a giant strip of bacon. *(She laughs.)* Bacon to go with these fried eggs.

(Thunder rumbles in the distance.)

WOMAN: He's been my closest friend for the last twenty-three years. We were supposed to grow old together. But now, now, after all this, after twenty-three years we're alone? Alone together? How can that be? I never wanted to be alone. I thought I was always one step ahead of it. I fucked to escape it. Men I hardly knew, men I couldn't even stand. I spent entire nights drunk, blasting music, blindly fucking, anything to push out the loneliness. To drown it out. To weep it away. Friends? What friends? Disposable friends that could do nothing to help.

60

Nothing. I had a circle of prattling friends and still it found me anyway. Vast, silent, colossal, loneliness. It found a way back in and before I even knew it, it was that gigantic aloneness that I was sleeping next to. Letting fuck me night after night. I was being thrusted by solitude, pounded by despair. So raw so often that I turned off. I let myself go numb.

(Thunder rumbles closer.)

WOMAN: Alone together? How can that be?

(The sky begins to darken.)

WOMAN: What have I done to my life? What have I done to my life?

(A light rain begins to fall.)

WOMAN: How did I fuck up my marriage so badly!?

(The rain gently taps her on the head.)

WOMAN: THIS KIND OF SHIT WASN'T SUPPOSED TO HAPPEN TO ME!

(The sea does not care.)

WOMAN: What am I supposed to do? What don't I understand? What didn't we know to do? Now at... Now at the end. Now that we are dying?

Journey

Jean Stevens

Scene: here and now

Dramatic
Jenny: a single mom about to embark on a journey. 40s

> *Here, Jenny speaks of the joys and the pains of raising three kids all by herself.*

JENNY: I had no ch-ch-choice, really. Mary—Mother—had to go into a home. Even at the sheltered accommodation she couldn't take care of herself. I just couldn't cope.

After Steve left, I brought up the three kids on my own, I looked after pet rabbits, a gerbil, goldfish, even the bloody stick insects they brought home from school. I am sick of being a carer. I don't want to have any more things to weigh me down with love. I've got to try and have a life of my own, do silly things, be a person in my own right. Yes, yes, I know I *should* have been doing these things all along but *you* try juggling the needs three demanding kids, coping with scratty little part-time jobs, constantly being careful with money, seeing to all the things that needed doing in the house. Most of the time I was just plain knackered. These women who manage to do everything, well they must have some help, that's all I can say, but they don't half make you feel guilty.

D-d-don't get me wrong, I'm not moaning. I got married early, *chose* to have the kids, and most of the time I enjoyed being a mother but, but…if I had my time over again …

The two lads live away now, they've got their own lives. They don't ring up or write but that's okay you don't expect it from lads. I 'phone them and write to them and from what I can gather they're doing all right. John's got a good job in a solicitor's office, he likes it, he's on the way up. Peter's on the dole but he seems to have a good time with his mates, they all muck in. I think they all do jobs on the side which they don't declare and they always seem to have money for drinking, so, well, I suppose you've got to let them get on with it.

But don't give me all that crap about whatever they get up to it's somehow got to be the mother's fault. I brought those lads up just the same and look at the difference in them. I can't be responsible for them any more.

Sarah, well it's great to have a daughter, there's so much you can share. But, to tell you the truth, I don't think she ever got over Steve going. It's no joke losing your Dad. And it doesn't matter what I say, to this day she still thinks it was somehow her fault that he left. It's always given her a bit of an "edge." And now she seems to have got in with a crowd who try to make a profession out of being disillusioned. She says she has no ambitions, no dreams.

I'm not saying they don't have it hard—she's known nothing but crap governments and an uncaring society and nobody seems to give a damn whether they sink or swim. But she worries me, she's so dismissive of everything.

Well, I'm going to give this travel thing a go. If I d-d-dare. Don't laugh, but I've always wanted to go round the world. When I was a teenager, I hitchhiked round Europe. I loved it. And I was full of confidence, though I say it myself. I sort of vaguely thought I'd do some more traveling, go farther afield, test myself a bit more. It was very scary but I think I really would have done it. But, then… I met Steve. He was so…so… I fell head over heels for him, mooning about like a great daft cow.

Before I knew where I was, I was pregnant. We got married. I'm not sure I even thought it through. It just all seemed to follow a logical pattern. Then before I knew where I was, I had three kids, a sagging belly, no husband, no career, shit.

It wasn't that Steve was terrifically handsome, or clever, or anything. It was just that he could always make me laugh. When he went, I missed the sex, course I did, I missed the companionship, but more than anything I missed not falling about laughing at almost everything. I think since then I've got more and more po-faced and squeamish about what I laugh at, if I laugh at all. If only I could get...things...back.

N-n-now I'm just feeling...well, left behind, left out of it. What if I can't get things back? Oh, why the hell did I waste so much, or did I, or what, was it my fault, was it... Oh, dunno, I don't really want to go down that road.

Journey

Jean Stevens

Scene: here and now

Serio-Comic
Sarah: a bundle of nervous energy. 20

> *Jenny's daughter, Sarah, is the embodiment of her troubled generation. Here, she describes why she's left college and the restlessness that has her in its grasp.*

SARAH: Well, I've left the boyfriend. It was getting a bit much. He was beginning to sound like any minute he'd be coming out with phrases like "settle down" and "make a commitment." No, I'm doing him wrong there. He wouldn't talk bollocks like that. But I know he'd like us to be, well, together. I couldn't handle it. No, that's crap. Me! I can handle anything. But I just had to get away.

I had to leave college, too, 'cos I didn't want to keep bumping into him or his mates. It's no big deal, though, it wasn't going anywhere. College, I mean. Teacher training, what was I thinking about?! School holidays, I expect. But I'm buggered if I'm going to prostrate myself on the floor, flash my tits, crawl up the boss's arse, or whatever it is you have to do these days to be considered for a job. And then when you get there, if you're not set on fire by the students, or shot by some fucking nutter, you'll probably be stabbed by a junkie. They can stuff it. I've had a few interviews in my time and it's a sick joke. I think some of the bastards get their rocks off calling people in and giving them the third degree when there isn't a cat in hell's chance of employing them. Don't know what I'll do. I'll chill out at home, see what happens.

That was a turn up for the books, old Jenny thinking of going off round the world with a rucksack on her back. Bloody hell. It's true what they say, you go away from home and when you come back the person who stands in front of you isn't your Mum any more she's some woman with a life. Except I don't think she thinks she has a life. So join the club.

Anyway, Jenny's got this bee in her bonnet and I think she should get it out of her system. Get the bee in her bonnet out of her system?? Wouldn't think I was an English student, would you? Not that it matters. What a stupid subject to choose. Like they said, better get your head round Business Studies and Information Technology, there's no place for poetry round here. Or, of course, you could always think about teaching. Ha! Ha!

I just hope Jenny does go and "find herself" or we'll never hear the end of it. If we don't watch out, it'll be nag, nag, nag, and it's all your fault I never had a chance.

Must keep in touch with the girls at college. My best friend Kelly has this sort of bet on. She's keeping a chart based on the news. It's stuck on her wall and she fills it in every day. So many points for murders, so many for child abuse, so many for wars, so many for road rage, so many for rapes and muggings—and so on.

If it gets to the end of this month and the chart's not full she's going to hitch-hike to France. But, if it is full, she's going to take an overdose. Cool, eh!

We played Russian Roulette once. Not with guns—we couldn't get hold of any. Well, we could, but the price was too high. Instead of five blanks and a bullet, we had five red cards and the Ace of Spades. The atmosphere was all wrong, though. I wanted it to be all tense and dramatic and I propped the window open so as soon as you got the Ace you had to leap straight out and five floors down.

But Julie kept spoiling it by giggling. She wouldn't have giggled if we'd had a loaded gun.

That was when I knew he was getting a bit too serious. Saying he didn't like me playing dangerous games. And he gave me a whasscall. By a whasscall I mean, well, I suppose you'd have to call it a love letter. And a poem. It wasn't one he'd written himself. Absolutely not. He's not a nerd. No, it was that one by Oscar Wilde. I couldn't bear it.

I must go and see old Mary. Jenny's being a tad defensive about her. Apparently, she's…she's not like Gran any more. She was good to me, Mary. I can honestly say there wasn't one time she let me down. Not one. You can't say that for most people.

She'd meet me after school and we'd always have something special for tea. The boys'd be off somewhere else so it was always Gran and me. She'd hide things round the house. Daft bugger, she had a little saying: "Always believe there'll be summat good round the corner." Daft old cow.

But in Mary's house there always was something good. She'd do the old thing, you're cold, you're cold, you're getting warm, and suddenly in the silliest of places you'd find a bar of chocolate, a new bit of Lego, something daft like an old clothes peg made into a doll. When she had no money at all, she'd hide one of those things you make out of newspaper. You know, you fold the paper together, then cut round it and when you open it out it's children holding hands and dancing, that sort of thing.

I've not seen Gran for a bit, but I'm not going to feel guilty, guilt is for Jenny. Anyway, Mary'll understand. She always told me to "Go for it." Except I went for it, and it wasn't there.

God, I feel restless.

I went out this morning and ran thirty-five times round the block. Me! You wouldn't catch me dead doing the poncy health club thing—in the gym with the lycra-clad lovelies and the muscle-bound wankers. I didn't go out for a jog, I just went out, and suddenly there I was racing round and round like a mad cat in a thunderstorm. Couldn't help it.

Journey

Jean Stevens

Scene: here and now

Dramatic
Mary: once a vibrant woman, now battling senility in a nursing home. 70s

> *Here, Mary speaks of her daughter, Jenny, and granddaughter, Sarah, as well as her frustration with her lack of control over body and mind.*

MARY: Hello. There is somebody still in here, tha knows. That's what we always used to say: tha knows. Until our Jenny got a bit posh and used to tell me off for it. She had pretensions then. I don't blame her but I don't think you can shake off your roots and all that quite so easily.

Anyway, I'm in here and I'm trapped. Like my body's got a mind of its own. I should be so lucky! Get a bit frightened. Like I go on a journey and I can't get myself back. Yesterday, I found roses and lilies and the gold of the world. And the shimmer and glow just out of reach. And I yearned and I wept and I held out my hands and… What? Oh, it's hard trying to think these days. What's that phrase they use? I can't quite…get…it…together.

They shove pills at me, day in and day out, nobody's ever told me what they are or what they're for.

Way they look at me you'd think they were ready to smack me any minute for nothing at all, let alone if I dared to say something. The other day this doctor came slumming round here. He looked all of twelve. What does he do, he pats me on the head. I felt like saying if I wanted a pat on my head, I'd ask a cow. But the words got all muddled and stuck in my throat.

Our Jenny's been trying to explain something to me. Says she's off to…where was it? I wasn't even that close to her, but I felt her trembling. I couldn't get my head round it but I knew it was important. And I got all excited... I could feel my bones tingle and, if I'd waved my fingers, flames would have shot out. Then they turned that blasted telly up, and the poetry and the passion of dreams was drowned in absolute rubbish.

My only child, Jenny. We waited a long time for her. And after her no more babies came.

They say only ones are spoiled, don't they. I don't know what they mean by that. Do they mean it's better to treat 'em badly? They have phrases for these things, don't they, like over-protection. Well, maybe I did over-protect her. But it's a damn sight better than under-protecting her, in my book.

But, in a way, I don't think Jenny was ready for real life, and she took it very hard having to cope on her own. She's never really believed in herself. Perhaps I always expected too much. All my eggs in one basket. She couldn't come up to scratch.

I wish she hadn't dumped me here. I'd like to be with her. I'd like her to say...

I don't like the scrap heap. Heck, what? Can't remember where I was. It all went into a big blur.

That Sarah, my granddaughter, now she's a different kettle of fish. I hardly understand her language sometimes. Not that I've seen her recently. She's off at college. She's going to be a teacher. A nice profession for a young lady. And she's got a boyfriend. I'd like to see her settled down.

And I reached out for glory and found only dust...

I don't like these folks in here. Not a bit. No. They're old. And there's one old dear makes a positive point of charging into you with her zimmer frame.

She used to make fun of me, Sarah. I'd be telling her something about myself, something real serious, and all she'd say would be: *(Mary does a fair imitation of Sarah.)* "Yeah, yeah, yeah—we know, in your day, you walked ninety miles to school in your bare feet through ten foot snow drifts. Yeah, yeah, yeah, when you lived in a paper bag..."

Sarah hadn't a clue. My mam and dad died young, I brought

the others up and fended for myself, I lived through the Depression, and the war. And there was…Bob…he was with me and we lived in the light and laughed in the rain…and then the war came…and they killed him…and… You never love again, not like the first time. Jack was a treasure, a good husband, but he wasn't Bob.

You can't tell Sarah anything. She thinks she's the only one to see any bad times. You have to fight, you have to get on with it. You have to be on the side of life. But try and tell her that and you get the "paper bag" routine. I love her to bits. It's like the more she does silly things, like all this—whadycallit—"dropout stuff," the more I love her. She reminds me of myself sometimes. I was always doing things on the spur of the moment. Like I'd have so much energy I didn't know where to fling myself next.

And now, I'm stuck here. Like a little bag of bones in dirty carpet slippers.

Killer Joe

Tracy Letts

Scene: a trailer home on the outskirts of Dallas, Texas

Dramatic
Dottie: a simple young woman caught up in dangerous circumstances. 18–20

> *Dottie's father and brother have hired Joe to kill her mother*
> *for the insurance money. Joe, in turn, has demanded time*
> *with Dottie as partial payment for the deed. Here, Dottie tells*
> *the killer a horrifying tale of her mother.*

DOTTIE: My momma tried to kill me when I was real little. She put a pillow over my face and tried to stop me from breathing, cause she cared more about herself than her little baby, and she didn't love me like a mother loves a little baby. And she thought she'd done it, and she was happy, cause then she didn't have to worry about me eating her food, and sleeping in her bed, and growing up to be the part of her that was cut out and grown into a better thing than she had been, had ever been. Cause that would mean the best part of her was me. But she hadn't done it, she didn't give me back to Him, she only made me sick, made me not be for a while, but then I was and she was sad that I was, and that I always would be.

Lemon Meringue Façade

Ted Lange

Scene: Los Angeles

Comedic
Susan: a woman with unique insight into human reproduction. 20s–30s

> *When a gathering of friends brings on the inevitable bashing of men, Susan speaks with humor and wisdom about the nature of sperm.*

SUSAN: Let me draw you a picture. One you probably never thought of. Men have a couple of thousand sperm.

[PHYLLIS: Millions, You mean a couple of million.]

SUSAN: Okay, a couple of million. Let's say that your egg is the prize at the end of the race.

[PHYLLIS: Naturally. I have no say in this stupid contest. If they want a prize give them a Lexus. Let'um race around in that for a while.]

SUSAN: Could you just follow my train of thought for a minute? Phil why do you think they have millions of sperm racing for one egg?

[PHYLLIS: Hello! That's the sixty-four dollar question.]

SUSAN: We, women have the power and most of us just don't realize it. But men do. They're really afraid of us. The sperm dance is a real weak step. Phyllis just imagine all those guys lined up at the starting gate, and all they've got to do is race one hundred yards. Hell, half of them fall down before they even get out of the gate.

[PHYLLIS: I must confess, I've had my share of those.]

SUSAN: Now you've only got half a million left. Then you lose ninety percent of them before they get to the five yard line They are tripping all over each other trying to get to the egg, some are down and winded trying to suck in more air. Others have just given up, turned around and are wandering home. A lot of them wonder what the hell they're even doing on the track. That's how dumb they are.

[PHYLLIS: They sound like soap opera actors.]

(The sound of a toilet flushing.)

SUSAN: Not everybody makes it to the finish line. If you were to stand at the end of the one hundred yards…You would see a pile up of sperm, bunched together trying to figure out where the egg is. Two or three crawl out of that mess and start running. But I'll be damned if they know less about running, than they do about fertilizing. So those three guys are running off in every direction but the right direction. By the time they get their bearings there is only one guy down there near the egg and he can't figure out how to get in.

Lemon Meringue Facade

Ted Lange

Scene: Los Angeles

Serio-Comic

Linda: a white woman faced with the challenge of raising a bira-
cial baby. 30s

> *When her African American friend, Richard, goads Linda by
> questioning her understanding of the realities of raising a bi-
> racial child, she lets him have it…so to speak.*

LINDA: Are you finished? I hope you're finished. Because I don't
want to be interrupted.

[RICHARD: I'm finished.]

LINDA: Let me tell you something Mr.-I'm-blacker-than-you'll-ever-
be. I don't give a fuck what you think; or what my Mother thinks,
or what that asshole that used to be my husband thinks. THIS
CHILD IS MINE! I helped conceive her, I carried her, and I brought
her into this world. She is my daughter, for better or for worse,
I'm her Mother. You fucking men. You bury your dick in us and
all of a sudden you're an authority on women. True, I may not
know what it's like to be black, or half black. I know next to nothing about the African-American culture. I'm not even sure who
Malcolm TEN was.

[RICHARD: MALCOLM X.]

LINDA: Malcolm X, Malcolm Ten, whatever. I know I've got a lot to
learn. I don't know what this façade shit is you're talking about,
But if it's coming down, let the motherfucker come down. Am I
putting this in terms that you can understand, Dick? And, it better do it soon, cause I got a whole lot of work to do. I'm going
to raise my daughter.

It took me seven years of trying, three years of fertility exper-
iments and a trip to Jamaica. I have my child. I'm going to love

my child. More than any thing else I'm going to love Roberta. With that as our foundation; the façade can do whatever the fuck it wants. We will meet it head on. Together.

The Lesson

Michael D. Sepesy

Scene: a classroom

Serio-Comic
Mrs. Hogan: a junior high school teacher who has just received some bad news. 20–50

> *Here, bitter Mrs. Hogan gives the girls in her class a lesson they will never forget.*

MRS. HOGAN: …and that is the miracle of life.

Okay, girls. Umm. That's sex. That's the science of it, at any rate. *(Thinks, nervous.)* Umm. I don't know why I'm doing this, but…sex is a very personal thing, and I would feel remiss if I didn't cover the personal side. Sex is a beautiful gift from God… except when it's between two people. I'm sorry. That's wrong. I mean, sex is a beautiful gift from God between two people… except when one of those people is a man. No. I'm sorry. That's not fair. I just got some very bad news this morning. *(Brings out Barbie doll.)* Here's you, the woman. Let's call her Unwitting Dupe. Okay? She lives in a little dreamland where she reads romance novels and *Cosmo* and believes somewhere out there there's a man for her who'll respect her for her mind, sweep her away and rip her bodice on a bed of rose petals to the songs of Johnny Mathis. She's not stupid, just misled. She's got her hopes and wishes and goals.

Here's the man. He's here to crush all that. You can tell he's a man because of the remote control. The only thing that separates a man from the apes is his ability to change channels from a distance with his little couch scepter, his electronic pseudo-phallus. So here's our man. Let's call him Screwtape…because he's the Devil…he's a demon from Hell and his only mission in life is to murder your soul. Not all at once. That wouldn't be evil enough.

But inch by inch, in small ways. Like forgetting your birthday. Or belittling what you do in front of his friends. "Oh, that little teaching job of hers, ha ha ha." Or making you cry on your wedding night by calling you by someone else's name. Or waiting right before you have to come to school and talk about relationships to give you some devastating personal news. Just as an example.

How does it start, you ask? Well, one day, Unwitting Dupe finds herself walking around the college campus, her head in the clouds. *(Singing, as Barbie.)* "Some day my prince will come…Oh. Hello, Screwtape. Would you like to talk about logical positivism?" *(As ape.)* "Let's fornicate." Suddenly you're in his van with your ankles over your ears, and he's trying out all this fancy shmantzy stuff he got from dirty movies during his misspent puberty. So much for romance. But you figure things will get better. After all, the hard part is over. You've found a man. As if that was some kind of accomplishment.

Then Prince Charmless whisks you away and you get married, and at the end of the ceremony, they put a big saddle on you so Mighty Joe can ride you like a two dollar mule. "Giddyup, wife! Hi ho, Maid Service, away!" And you gallop off into the sunset of indentured servitude, where for the next fifteen years all you get to hear is this: *(As ape.)* "Cook! Where's my lunch? Where's my Hasenpfeffer?"

What Screwtape doesn't realize is that the reason his dinner is late is you had to throw away the first batch because it was laced with Drano. *(Singing.)* "Some day my prince will die…" *(Has Barbie pick up scissors.)* Isn't that right, Screwtape? You want to swing from the trees, monkey boy? Try swinging with that little bitch from packaging you've been fucking for five years!

(She's about to plunge the scissors into the gorilla when a bell rings.)

MRS. HOGAN: Okay. That's the end of the period. Remember to read chapter seventeen over the weekend. Bye, girls. Have fun in Home Ec.

The Little Oasis

Lora Lee Ecobelli-Amram

Scene: an antebellum mansion in the foothills of the Blue Ridge Mountains of northern Virginia

Serio-Comic

Madeline: a woman suddenly confronted with her past. 40s

> *Madeline has been reunited with John, her high school sweetheart, by an odd set of circumstances. Seeing John again brings back happy memories from their youth as she here relates.*

MADELINE: Mmmnn…I bet you don't remember the night we saw the meteorite shower. You had just finished writing that book of poetry. I was so impressed. I had never met a boy who wrote anything before, let alone poetry! I remember, you pulled over at Stony Man lookout and that's where we saw them. *"Like angels dancing across in the sky," you said. (She pauses to savor the memory.)* I can still see you standing up in the back of the truck, a little bit tipsy, shouting verse up to the sky. Words so strong and pure that they echoed across the valley. Do you remember what you wished for that night?

> [*(John picks up a small stone and throws it violently against the house leaving Madeline shocked at his abrupt mood change. There is an uncomfortable pause in which Madeline is not sure whether she should stay or flee.)*]

MADELINE: Oh my word, I am so embarrassed! You must think I am nothing but a sentimental old fool.

Mad Maenads (Wives)

Victoria Charkut

Scene: a restaurant

Serio-Comic
Mirella: a woman questing for meaning in her life. 20s–30s

> *While she waits for her pasta, married Mirella enjoys a favorite fantasy.*

MIRELLA: I want to go to Africa.

I want to sit in the hot sun and have a Zulu man come and make love to me.

I often think about Africa. The emptiness. The grass like wheat, waving, caressing. The openness, the animals running by. I love giraffes. Well, I think I love them. I've never smelt one, of course. Maybe they smell awful. That's something I'd have to find out.

In my dreams, I see myself walking in Africa, walking across the golden plain in a long white muslin dress, or sometimes I'm wrapped in that batik material, dark inky-indigo blue, with nothing on underneath and soft leather sandals. And a white parasol for the intense heat.

No safari outfits for me. No way. I'd be protected by my princes.

One hot afternoon when I'm all alone, having sent everyone away, I lie by a green lake, and while watching the elephants in the distance drinking the cool water, my Zulu man comes, very quietly, stands over me looking down with his huge brown eyes. His muscles gleam in the bits of sunlight that filter down through the trees.

I tell him my name, but he smiles and puts his finger to my lips so I won't speak. He offers me a cool drink, a strange-tasting drink that we drink together (out of a gourd or something) and then I become heady and light, like a beautiful white bird that he has to catch, needs to catch. And then my Zulu man lifts me....lifts me...right up...on to...

Mad Maenads (Wives)

Victoria Charkut

Scene: a restaurant

Serio-Comic
Mirella: a woman questing for meaning in her life. 20s–30s

> *Mirella has recently been seen by a past-life regressionist. Here, she reveals her former identity to a friend over lunch.*

MIRELLA: As you may or may not remember, I recently got into crystals. Remember when I went and housesat for Stewart and Michael? They have those birds, you know. Earl had to go to Atlantic City for two weeks. So I spent a week in Topanga Canyon, this little house filled with sunshine and crystals. Crystals in white sand by the windows, huge crystals on either side of the bed, crystals all around the bathtub. In the living room they had a black coffin. (*Gestures "Don't ask me!"*)

So then, I started buying books on crystals and books on being a warrior. "Pain and depression" being great "source materials for transformation." I had a goldmine there.

Meanwhile I was receiving this newsletter from two women who own this crystal shop—I don't know how they got my address or name. Maybe I bought a book there…anyway…during this extreme period of anxiety, pain and depression, I decide to take one of their workshops called: "Meet Your Self in Your Past Life."

[TONYA: No. Like, wow.]

MIRELLA: Mmm…Of course, I'd often thought about this like everyone else, for about two minutes. I'd see myself in Egypt, riding camels swathed in red silk. Lying back on satin pillows at Roman banquets…surrounded by cherubini feeding me oysters and caviar, pomegranates and zabaglione. The courts of Paris where painters begged to replicate my soft white body.

So.

I found myself at this workshop and with the help of Dolores and Mindy, and this very tall man with a long beard, I found out that in my former life…I was…ta daaaaaaaaa… *(Progressively going into a northern English accent.)* …a big huge dirty foul-mouthed coal miner in northern England in the late 1800s.

Fascinating hmmm?

The more we worked on me the more it all started coming back. The stroll home at night wi' me mates, laughin' and rippin' apart them tight-arsed Tories. Scrubbin' and scrubbin' the black from hands and face an hour every night so's the wife would serve the supper without complainin'. All the whingin' she made me listen to because I was too tired on Saturday nights for anything but a few lagers with the lads down at the Cock and Pheasant. And that afternoon down the shaft when Andy McPherson and I got carried away. Well. It was all there. I found out everything.

So. Now I have this…new knowledge…this sort of solid support instead of all those dreams about being a leader of fashion in the Imperial courts of Prussia, decked out in sparkling emeralds, rubies, opals, and amethysts, Rasputin waiting outside my door… Alfred was me name. Alfred Dunnock.

It explains a few things. Like why I've always been obsessed with pickled onions and insisted on coal heating.

Mad Maenads (Wives)

Victoria Charkut

Scene: a restaurant

Serio-Comic
Tonya: a philosophically unfaithful wife. 20s–30s

Here, earthy Tonya extols the perks of extramarital activity.

TONYA: Go ahead and tell me you wouldn't like to find him in your pajamas one morning.

[(Mirella says nothing.)]

TONYA: Yup, that's about it. Marriage. Can't live with 'em, can't debowel them. Maybe if you're Julie Andrews and, what's-his-name, in your… *(Julie Andrews voice.)* "Malibu mansion-by-the-sea, with your yacht and a cup of tea…" maybe then it's different. I don't know. Some guy, I forget his name but he said,

"Marriage is like a big castle up on this hill and all the people who aren't married are looking up at the castle wanting to get up there and get in! And all the people who are married, the ones in the castle are looking down trying to figure how to get the hell out." Or at least find a back door to sneak out once in a while. That's it in a nutshell babe. Maybe Mel Brooks and Anne Bancroft have it down but…I lie there next to him at night, when we're going off to sleep, and as his breath goes into me and mine back into him, night…after night…after night…after night…I wonder if this breathing of each others' breath isn't just a little too intimate, a little too addictive. If…I could possibly, if I ever wanted to I mean, shake myself free of this, this dependency, this entwinement. It's like our souls are so mingled, intertwined that we've become these thick hard roots of some great old tree. This sounds stupid right?

[MIRELLA: No. Go on.]

TONYA: I had to find out if other men's…breath…was AS IMPORTANT.

How...*weighty* it was. It's potential to soothe me. Their touch, not just sex, their touch. And I found out! It's like electricity. It's like sticking your finger into an electrical outlet!

It's better than wine, restaurants, vitamins! Mirella, it's better than shopping.

When I think of all those wasted faithful years. I was completely faithful for ten years Mirella. Ten years! Just look at me now! I've lost thirteen pounds Mirella. Have you ever seen me look this happy? Have you?

Monica: A Contemporary Monologue

Michael Hemmingson

Scene: here and now

Serio-Comic
Woman: a woman who thinks she's Monica Lewinsky. 20–30

> *Here, a conservative preacher's wife reveals some shocking dreams she's had about some famous people in Washington, D.C.*

WOMAN: Something weird is going on. *(Pause.)* I think I'm Monica Lewinsky. *(Pause.)* I mean, I think something weird is going on with the time-space continuum, something bizarre is going on within the shift of our dimension, inside the very fabric of our connected souls, so that somehow my soul, my beautiful soul, is inside both my body and the body of Monica Lewinsky.

We look alike. *(She holds up a magazine with Lewinsky's picture, smiles like her, holds the picture to her face.)* You see. The strange ways of God. This woman right here, this woman, is me.

I mean, I might be a right-wing born-again Christian, but I've secretly always wanted to be a liberal intern with political aspirations, walking the halls of the White House and getting to know—if you know what I mean by *know*—all the right people.

To tell you a real secret, ever since 1993 I've had these reoccurring erotic dreams that I'm having sex with Bill Clinton. Well, not exactly sex. I give Clinton blow jobs in these dreams. This doesn't happen in the Oval Office, but in some seedy cheap motel room. We rendezvous, Bill and I, under assumed names—his Secret Service men take care of all the details. These are really interesting dreams. *(Pause.)* So when I, when I saw Monica Lewinsky on the TV, and I heard about the blow jobs she was giving Clinton in the Oral Office, I said, "Jesus Christ Lord and Savior, help me, for there goes my beating heart." *(Pause.)* All these memories started flooding into my head. Massive déjà vu. I remember being in the Ovum Office with Bill.

I was living a double-life!

This could by why my husband and I have been playing these games lately. We've been playing Bill & Monica. He's Bill, and I'm Monica, naturally.

"Oh, Monica!" he says. "Monica, you are so young and pretty!"

"Oh Bill!" I say. "Mr. President, you are so handsome and powerful!"

"The pressures, Monica!" he says. "The pressures of being the Leader of the Free World."

"What can I do to help, Mr. Clinton?" I say.

And so my husband takes his penis out, and he says, "You can help me with this Monica. I have a very high-pressure meeting with the Senate today, and I need relief."

"Oh yes! Mr. President!" I say. I get down on my knees and say, "I will do anything, Mr. President, to help keep the world clean for democracy!"

This has helped our marriage. *(Pause.)* But you know, I had this weird dream last night, that just enforces my belief that I'm Monica Lewinsky. In this dream, I was Monica Lewinsky, and I was taking a stroll through a park with Bill Clinton, when all of the sudden these aliens, these ugly, thug like aliens, come down, and they wanted to beat up Bill for some reason. "We are gonna kick your white earthling ass," they said. I jumped in front of Bill, I smiled and opened my blouse like so, and I said, "Hey, maybe I can do something to help."

I realized this was a big mistake. These were eight-feet tall ugly aliens, galactic thugs, with this oozing gray skin, like they were dying of something.

Bill and I ran. We ran into the White House and tried to hide. There was this big party happening in the White House. Hillary gave me a glass of white wine and said, "Take a load off, Monica," but it kinda sounded like, "Suck a load out, Monica."

There were a lot of people at this party. One of the aliens followed us in. Everyone was quite flabbergasted. I ran into a bathroom and didn't lock the door in time. The alien had forced his way in with me. We looked at each other. I grabbed a piece of soap. I wanted to hit him. Instead, I began to wash him.

"I love you," I said to the alien.

"And I love you," said the alien.

We kissed. It was quite a kiss. I mean, weird, because as we kissed, the alien started to turn into this half-man, half-dog, and half-frog. A man-dog-frog that was now six feet tall and kissing me. It was still quite a passionate kiss. It stripped me naked. It wrapped its hind legs around my waist and its penis was hard and it started to have sex with me.

The sex was so—frantic! And hard. We broke the bathroom door down. We fell into the White House party and went away at it with everyone around watching. Our passion was divine. Hillary was refreshing everyone's drink.

Then, when the alien was done, other people started to have sex with me. I didn't try to stop them. It was exciting. Because I was having sex with famous people.

I had sex with Ted Kennedy, and that was weirder than having sex with the alien dog-man-frog. I had sex with CNN Correspondent Wolf Blitzer. "Blitz me baby!" I went. "Blitz me good!" Jesse Helms screwed me in the ass while Bob Dole pissed in my hair. Rush Limbaugh sucked on my tits and George Stephanopolus was dressed like a little girl and saying, "Mommy, Gerogina has been bad and needs to be spanked!" Then Al Gore showed up, with this huge hard-on, and he said, "Monica, I want one of those famous blow jobs that you give Bill!" He said, "My semen is very healthy, Monica, because I only eat organic food and I'm environmentally sound."

After they were all done with me, I sat on a couch with a naked Hillary Clinton. Hillary kissed me and licked all the semen and sweat off me. Far away, somewhere, I could hear Bill saying my name, softly, so softly:

"Monica, oh Monica…" *(Pause.)* They have some wild parties in Washington, D.C., that's all I can say.

I haven't told my husband about this dream. He's a pastor in our church, so he might not understand.

It's my little secret. *(Pause.)* I wonder if Monica Lewinsky dreams about my life.

Murmurs of California

Robert Vivian

Scene: an upscale restaurant

Dramatic
Kate: a woman seeking escape from her life. 30s

> *Kate and her father share a fantasy of driving to California. When her husband insists that California is only a metaphor for the ultimate escape from life's responsibilities, she angrily reminds him that they've been there before.*

KATE: You have the balls to say such a thing in front of me, in front of us, when you know how special our relationship is, what a little girl I am deep down inside, how I've loved you all these years, how I've supported you, believed in you, how he takes you out and buys you clothes and drinks and CDs and dinners…

[JACK: *(Looking around.)* I can't hear a fucking word in this place. Where's that goddamned waiter?]

KATE: We've been there before! Don't you remember? Don't you ever think about it? It was the best time of my life. I'll never forget the first time I drove on the freeway. You were out of town somewhere with your family. It was the first time I was all alone in Los Angeles. I creeped up to the Ventura onramp until the light was green. I had the window down. I was listening to a disco station. I got on the freeway and started speeding. I was flying by people! I was going so fast! And I thought, This is the beginning of my life! This is the beginning of my real life, the one I was always meant to live! The palm trees were glistening, the sun was straight up in the sky, I didn't see one face or car I knew and I turned the music all the way up! All the way up! *(Pause.)* Three months later we came back here. Sometimes I think I'll never see the sun again.

Office Hours

Norm Foster

Scene: a psychiatrist's office

Serio-Comic
Sharon: a beleaguered shrink. 30–40

> *When her patient crawls out on the window ledge, Sharon finds that she's in the middle of a schedule crisis.*

SHARON: Neil?… Neil, come inside, would you please? I mean, I've worked very hard to build up a good reputation in the psychiatric community, Neil, and it's not exactly a feather in my cap to have a nut on my ledge? Not that you are a nut, I'm not saying you're a nut. You're just experiencing an intellective setback. *(Checks her watch.)* Neil, please, my four o'clock is going to be here any minute. Your time is up. If you stay out there any longer, I'm going to have to charge you for the whole hour… All right, Neil, listen. I'm going to share something personal with you. If I share something personal with you, will you come in? You see, I'm unattached, Neil. Extremely unattached. What I'm trying to say is, I…I haven't been…with a man for over a year. That's right, twelve months, Neil. And that causes anxiety. Frustration. I mean, I'm as frustrated as an Avon Lady in Mennonite country. And very tense. I'm very tense these days. Yesterday I picked a fight with a Goodwill canvasser. But that's about to change, Neil. Oh, yes. You see, a couple of weeks ago I met a man. A nice man. A man I really like. And he likes me. And this afternoon at five o'clock, we're going away to a secluded lake, and do you know what we're going to do all weekend, Neil? Well, let's put it this way. If the cabin's rockin', don't bother knockin'. So, what do you say, Neil? How 'bout you just get the hell inside, huh?

[NEIL: *(Offstage.)* Would you be quiet in there?! I'm on the phone with my mother!]

SHARON: You're what? *(She looks out the window.)* You've got a phone out there?! Oh, for God's sake. Well, that does it. That does it! Now hear this, Neil. I am leaving at five o'clock sharp, and if you're not off that ledge by then, one way or the other, then you are locked in for the weekend, buster!

Our Lady of Perrysburg

Sherry Camp Paulsen

Scene: a small town in Georgia

Serio-Comic
Bernice: an earthy homemaker and keeper of local lore. 30–50

> *Here, loquacious Bernice tells the sad tale of a local man who managed to freeze to death in August.*

BERNICE: Whoda thunk a person could freeze to death on the hottest day in August.

[MARIAM: He froze to death in August?]

BERNICE: Poor ol' Homer, he'd been savin' up for one of them there tractors with the air-conditioned cabs. Summer 'fore last, he finally got hisself enough money together to buy Bobby Mossings' used one over to Fremont. *(Beat.)* Oh, he was so proud up there ridin' high. Like I said, it was a hot day, a hundred and one in the shade, and he done had that air-conditionin' turned up full blast. Fool. Best Doc Ballard could guess, the gauge got stuck and kept lowerin' the temperature to dang near freezin'. It was such a small space inside that cab, and it got cold so fast, Homer done caught hisself that hyperthemia and died. *(Beat.)* Just did a slooooow freeze over about four miles. *(Points out the window.)* See that nice little *cleared* area over to the far side of the yard?

[MARIAM: Yes?]

BERNICE: *(Nods.)* Ol' Homer. Mowed a path clear through five farms 'for he runned outta gas. *(Beat.)* They had to pry him off his steerin' wheel. Ol' Homer, he come out stiff as a popcicle, he did.

Our Lady of Perrysburg

Sherry Camp Paulsen

Scene: a small town in Georgia

Serio-Comic
Bernice: an earthy homemaker and keeper of local lore. 30–50

> *Life can take some unexpected turns as illustrated here by Bernice.*

BERNICE: None of our mamas had spoken more'n two words to each other since we girls was in third grade.

[MARIAM: So, what happened?]

BERNICE: Well, it was all working out just fine till Giddy's gramma come outa her coma.

[MARIAM: Coma?]

BERNICE: Yeah, see Giddy's gramma'd been under since she'd got baptized late in life that previous spring. When she hit that cold lake water, she done went into a coma right there on the beach. *(Beat.)* Wouldn't ya know Giddy's gramma'd picked the very day we was to go to Atlanta to come outta her dang coma. Giddy's mama called every blame person in the county she knowed that morning, includin' all our mamas.

[MARIAM: Bummer.]

BERNICE: Yep. Jus' one more day and history woulda been rewrit. Why, George, couldn'ta helped to notice me in my hot pants. He'd a never fallen for that Patty Boyd and messed with all them drugs. *(Beat.)* I'da been Mrs. George Harrison! *(Pause.)* Bernice... Eulaila...Strunk...Harrison. *(Beat.)* Gotta right nice ring to it, don't it?

[MARIAM: Yeeeaaah.]

BERNICE: Oh well, can't complain. I did end up with Cap, after all.

Our Lady of Perrysburg

Sherry Camp Paulsen

Scene: a small town in Georgia

Serio-Comic
Mary: the mother of Jesus. Any age

> *Mary has made an unexpected appearance in Perrysburg. Here, the eternal Madonna and Bernice swap tales and wisdom.*

MARY: Oh, pleeeeease with the ever virgin! I've had to live with "virgin" tagged to my name for nearly two thousand years, now! *(Pouts.)* Hunh, Mary Magdelan, she got to be a saint but, oh no, *she* didn't have to be a *virgin!* It's not fair!

[BERNICE: It 'idn't?]

MARY: Bernice, I never got to have a normal life. *(Beat.)* I've always been a…"virgin mother." *(Beat.)* I'm an oxymoron, for crying out loud! *(Beat.)* I never got to be…to be…

[BERNICE: One of the girls?]

MARY: Yeah…one of the girls. *(Beat.)* Someone with the same wants and needs as any other woman. *(Beat.)* Everybody has this preconceived notion of who the mother of God *ought* to be and they won't see me any other way!

[BERNICE: Ain't you told nobody how you really feel?]

MARY: Oh, I have tried with Dolly, but she can't get past the Mary that appeared to Bernadette at Lourdes and the children at Fatima. I had a very *different* message in those days…with the halo and all that light streaming out of my hands, talking about suffering and penance. *(Beat.)* But I've changed so much since then! My message, my hair…these Birkenstocks! *(Beat.)* I thought I could get that across to Dolly…thought that standing in her birdbath would give me a more organic sort of appeal, but she just saw it as a pedestal!

[BERNICE: Well, why don't you just tell ever'body all at once? Get you one of them "infomercials" on TV.]

MARY: That's not kosher. Even Jesus didn't talk to *everybody* all at once after he died. Just me and the *other* Mary and his buddies, the disciples. *(Beat.)* Think about it, Bernice. If everybody could appear at *will* after death…faith would lose it's meaning entirely.

Plastic

Bill McMahon

Scene: here and now

Serio-Comic
Mona: a woman obsessed with her appearance. 20–30

Here, Mona describes her journey to becoming the perfect plastic woman.

MONA: What do you think when you hear the word "plastic"? Most people mean something negative nowadays. I don't remember just when "plastic" began to equal cheap and synthetic and phony. Sometime in the seventies, I suppose. When I was a little girl, plastic meant new, fresh, colorful, magical. Something from the future. Something exciting and wonderful. All of my best toys, all my favorite things around the house. Now people hear the word, and no matter how it's applied, whatever the context, it means something bad to them.

But, you see, they don't understand the word. Not really. They think they know what it means, but they don't. I looked it up in a very heavy, leather-bound, nonplastic dictionary, and I memorized the definition. Or definitions, since it means many things. Adjective: One, of material which changes shape when pressure is applied and retains its shape when the pressure is removed. Two: of the processes involved in using such materials to fashion things, i.e. *the plastic arts.* Three: of or relating to or characterized by three-dimensional movement, form, and space. Four: pliable, easily influenced. Five: unnatural, synthetic, so changeable as to be phony. Six: Noun, a plastic material.

Out of all that, just one definition that mentions phoniness, synthetics, negativity. Yet that is the meaning people carry with them. That's why I memorized the definition. I wanted people to know that calling me plastic is not, in my eyes, an insult. Not with all those other meanings. And I believe we should all have multiple meanings, more even than a leather-bound dictionary.

I am the plastic woman. I embrace all the definitions of plastic, save one. I believe I am now, in all of my plasticness, more naturally myself than I ever could have been otherwise. Because we create ourselves. That's what Mother taught me, and she, of all people, knew. Even if we do nothing to take part in the process, do not exercise our will over our physical and mental development, then that is a decision with consequences, too. And I wanted to take part. From my earliest days, I wanted to mold myself. I looked at my storybooks of Snow White, Sleeping Beauty, Cinderella, and Red Riding Hood, I watched Samantha and Jeannie and Mary Tyler Moore. And I knew. I knew what was desired and desirable. I knew what earned high grades. I knew fat was bad, thin was virtuous. Even being a little chunky was morally questionable. Being plain meant you weren't trying hard enough. I was not living in a child's fairy tale fantasy when I drew these conclusions. I was looking at the real world. I was looking at the world that rewarded what it looked at. Definition number four.

I tried so hard when I was young. I tried to be thin and pretty and pert. I wanted Mother to be proud of me. But no matter how many oreos or cupcakes I denied myself, it wasn't enough. Mother would heave a sigh of resignation when I presented myself for inspection every morning. It wasn't just that I had chosen the wrong blouse to go with the jumper, or that my socks were wrong for the shoes I'd chosen. It was the raw material that was wanting.

I feel delivered now. Delivered out of the ghetto of chunky, plain, aging people. People who are not special because no one expects them to be. People who don't test well. People who don't interview well. People who live limited, ordinary lives because nothing more is allowed or accorded. I don't advocate this view, I simply recognize it as a reality. And I move on. Definition number three.

I know you're all wondering what the first procedure was.

Those of you who guessed "nose" win the ribbon. There were, in fact, three separate procedures on the nose, the first of which was a little extreme and required some correcting. But I wasn't discouraged. I think I read in an art history text that Michelangelo actually believed the sculptures he carved existed within the uncarved stones and it was his job to free them—chipping away carefully at the slabs that imprisoned them. That has always been how I've thought about my surgeries—I'm just carving away the bits of me that aren't really me, that imprison me. I'm sculpting and molding. The plastic arts. Definition number two.

Cheek implants were next. My face used to have a flatness, a lack of definition. Saucer-shaped, blank. A blank tablet on which to begin my composition. I titled my composition "Top of the Class" because I wasn't going to be held back. I was going to excel. I was going to reform myself into the image that would place me in the top percentile. If I was to be an overachiever, I would first have to look the part. I would prove my worthiness by conforming to the standard. Responding to pressure, and retaining the shape of that pressure. Definition number one.

And what was my standard, you ask? What was that ultimate image that I held up as a standard? It wasn't Snow White or Samantha or even Audrey Hepburn. They were only two-dimensional, images of perfection projected on a flat surface. I needed a three-dimensional icon, someone with a sculptural presence. The perfect plastic being. *(She produces a Barbie Doll, holding it between her breasts like a sacred, cherished icon.)*

She was it. The most universal paradigm of beauty and grace. As firm, fresh and lovely as she was in 1959, the year she made her debut. And plastic, yes. Radiantly, triumphantly plastic in every sense. A standard for the modern woman to measure herself against. Yes, I hear you out there saying she was unrealistic, not even anatomically possible, a fantasy. But I tell you, an icon has no business being realistic. In fact, we want our icons, particularly our icons of beauty, to be as unrealistic, as distant as possible. Look at Michelangelo's *David*. Twice as unrealistic as Barbie ever thought of being, but the unrivaled standard of male beauty for centuries, and no one's argued about him being unnatural. David, on the contrary, is seen as heroic. I submit to you that Barbie is every bit as heroic in her way. Shouldn't there always be something more to strive for? I think I would die if I woke up one morning and had nothing left to work toward. I still have my first Barbie. Mother presented her to me on my eighth birthday. She has never been far from my mind or heart since. Barbie, I mean.

> [*(Two attendants enter, carrying gauze which they begin to wrap Mona with as she speaks to us.)*]

MONA: Someone who could not understand once said to me that my work-in-progress, my creation, represented nothing more or less than monumental self-hatred. I have to challenge that. It is self-love, not self-hatred, which propels me. I believe I am entitled to the best which life has to offer, and if appearances are unimportant, why not have the most highly polished? Why not be a more marketable commodity? I had a choice. Before I began my process, when I was not unpleasant but nevertheless ordinary looking, I was stuck in low-level, low-paying jobs and had limited social access. But once I began carving out my body and my identity, my world changed. Opportunities, professional and other, multiplied like hyperactive rabbits. Men became clay, as malleable in their way as I chose to be in mine. I now make six figures, and prospects are increasing all the time. All a matter of packaging. Nothing more, nothing less.

> [*(The attendants continue wrapping, covering her body in gauze, like a mummy. Mona stands perfectly still, clutching her Barbie.)*]

MONA: Yes, always striving for more. I stand before you the veteran of some twenty-eight plastic surgical procedures, and about to enter my twenty-ninth, a combination liposuction, breast, buttock, and eyelid lift which will bring me ever closer to my beloved goddess of perfection. I will be immobile for approximately eight to ten weeks, and yes, the pain will be severe. But nothing is achieved without cost.

> [*(The attendants, having wrapped her body, are now wrapping*

her head. Mona continues to speak to us, even as her eyes are covered.)]

MONA: There is always cost, whatever one's choices, and I have always been willing to pay. Years ago, as a child, Mother said something which at the time seemed harsh but which I would thank her for now, were she here to thank. We were shopping for dresses, and of course, I wanted the laciest, pinkest, most girlish creation on the rack. I ran to my mother holding my prize, but she said, "Your looks aren't right for that, Mona. It will make you look fatter and plainer. You need something simpler, less fussy. You need to know what you can carry off, and what you can't. We'll try to do something about your hair." Yes, it did feel like a slap in the face at the time, but Mother was doing me a favor, giving me a wake-up call from such an early age. I believe she would applaud my efforts now, had she not been the victim of a freak hair salon misadventure in 1973. Of course, we all now know never to follow a permanent wave with tint number five twenty-seven, but back then, well...but Mama knew the risks, and like myself, was always willing to pay the price. Her last words, just before she combusted, were "Never regret the pain or the inconvenience or the expense of improving yourself, Mona. First impressions. You are cast for life on the first impression." I'm sorry she isn't here to see me now, but I know I have her approval. In a way, she was carved from me, too. Along with the excess fat, two ribs and that nasty bit of cartilage. I have been streamlined by life and by design. *(Everything but her mouth is wrapped in gauze.)*

I know that my methods will always seem odd to some, but I ask only a small amount of flexibility in your thinking. Make your minds just a little plastic, a little pliable. Some form themselves from the inside out, but for me, a reverse process was necessary. The plastic arts. Definition number two. A journey toward self definition. One which has made me finally, completely, exhilaratingly, inexorably, consummately free.

A Pointless Story

Robert Vivian

Scene: here and now

Serio-Comic
Janice: a married woman who's had quite a day. 30s–40s

> *Janice's husband never in a million years expected to hear the following story*

JANICE: When I tell you what I have to tell you you'll no longer ignore me. Fair enough? You might even fall in love with me again, though God knows what that will mean.

I encountered a man on my walk. I asked him where he lived. I asked him to take me there. *(Pause.)* Do you believe that he took me there? Can you do that for just a second?

[*(He says nothing.)*]

JANICE: Good. You're speechless for once. He lived in a dive. The first thing I saw walking into his apartment was an empty can of peaches on the table. No curtains. One lamp without a shade. A spoon sticking out of the can. God knows how long it had been there. He said, "This is where I live," and I laughed in his face. But not on purpose. I said, "What a lovely place," and the odd thing is I really meant it: It *was* lovely because despite its threadbare appearance and utter lack of charm or comfort it was beautiful in its grime and filth. It had been lived in, kicked in, slept in, even eaten in by ants and maybe the occasional rat. At that point we were trying to read each other's mind. Mine said—I don't blame you for any of it: the empty can, the shadeless lamp, the damp and musty smell. We all have to make our accommodations. His said—Who is this lady and why is she here? I think I want to jump her. Which is exactly what he did after a few formalities.

[*(Hubby starts in his chair.)*]

100

JANICE: Keep your pants on. I didn't give in that easily. First a little conversation… No comments from the peanut gallery please.

[*(Hubby is sullen and chastised, waiting expectantly.)*]

JANICE: The room was so squalid, so beaten-in and abused that it was positively shocking in its neglect. I asked him, "How can you live this way?", not in censure, mind you, or disgust, but overwhelming curiosity. He sensed my sincerity and was immediately subdued—like a monk in his cave. He said, "I just let it go." How apt! How perfect! It was the first full answer I got out of him. I just let it go! As if that explained everything right down to the nitty-gritty. And it did, at least in his case and mine. I knew immediately we were pals, if not soul mates. I remember thinking, This is just the kind of man I've been looking for my whole life. Someone who accepts me without flinching. This is no reflection on you. You have responsibilities and we don't. All we have to worry about is our own state of mind, which is a full-time job. Anyway, we proceeded to the bedroom.

Don't be so dramatic. Nothing is what it seems. We went to the bedroom. He seemed to be gaining confidence. In fact, I think he began to understand the whole reason behind my visit, which wasn't the least bit carnal in intention but noble and searching in its own desperate way. Kind of like a visit from a sick relative who needed a change of venue for awhile.

He tried to take my hand and I wouldn't let him. "Are you crazy?" I said, and then we both began to laugh so hard that he pushed me on the bed and I threw a pillow at him. The push seemed gratuitous at the time but looking back at it now I guess he really wanted to get me on my back and who can blame him? He probably hadn't had a woman in his place for months, even years. Anyway, the pillow: hit him right in the chest and blew his hair back with a gust. He was shocked. I said, "Listen. I'm not here to do what you think we're going to do. I'm here to understand." That took the wind right out of him. He looked at me for a long time like he was going to choke me, then he looked confused and finally he looked lost. A whole kaleidoscope of emotions.

101

"Are you as hopeless as I am? Are you troubled?" I think he wanted to throw me out but he was mesmerized by my questions. I'm a snake charmer that way.

I said, "Why don't you come over sometime and meet my husband? We might make an impression on him together." Talk about angry. He nearly threw me out the window. He didn't want to hear about you anymore than if I had brought a vacuum to suck up all the dustballs. However. When he took his knife out of his pants—and it *was* a knife, not a metaphor for something else—I got angry. "Who do you think you are? Do you want to spoil a perfectly nice visit? We're not just a couple of fruitcakes here, we have problems we can face together. It's true I picked you out of a crowd, but what does that matter now? I like you all the same." *(Silence.)* The long and short of it was...he tried to attack me. He lunged for me on the bed but he didn't know I was a gymnast once as I rolled away and he knocked himself out on the headboard. Then I left. I was out of my mind. Briefly. Completely. I tried to see what another person was up to and I failed. I know. I'm a mess. But wait a minute. I went back to his place.

I said I went back. You're not listening. There he was sprawled out on his own bed and I grabbed some toilet bowl cleaner from his closet and stuck it under his nose. He came to with terror in his eyes and said, "You?" Then he let out a whimper and I couldn't help myself then and we ended up together after all in his dirty yellow bed, mating like two gazelles. I say gazelles because he had a long grimy neck and it was beautiful in a way and he fucked me like he wanted to and everything was going according to plan, never mind whose, etc., etc., etc. He fell asleep right next to me with his arm hanging off the bed. I remember thinking, Is this it? What have I done? A high-speed romp? I truly believe that was the low point of my life. He wasn't a lover, just someone I picked up because I was bored and sick of my life. So I saw the knife lying on the floor, catching the gleam of sunlight and I picked it up. I thought, What if I just stab him a few times? Just a couple of jabs between the ribs? He was fast asleep and his side looked like a sick deer's because whoever he was he didn't eat much. So I did; I stabbed him. Nothing fatal or remarkable. Of course there was a lot of blood, a lot of screaming. I told him to keep it down and take it like a man. But I got through to him. He huddled in the corner like a frightened child. "Listen," I said, shaking the knife like a nun with a ruler, "I didn't come here to be mounted by you. I came here to talk, pure and simple. Why do the simplest things have to get so nasty? All you thought the whole time was fuck, fuck, fuck, and I'm not fuck, I'm Janice. Couldn't you at least have asked me my name?" And this is what you have to realize, Hubby, this is what you must understand: No matter if I grow old with you or die today, most of my life has been pointless. And doesn't that bother you? The truth is I can't bear to be a part of the hypocrisy we've become involved in, which is that we're living together and for each other when in reality we're just living, drifting, allowing nothing of real consequence to move us, just living a series of half-assed entertainments that become unbearably dull the minute we stick the batteries in. You can stare all you want but the proof is in the pudding and the pudding is full of mushy pulp.

Pretzels and Longing

Linda Eisenstein

Scene: a bar

Serio-Comic
Maddie: a lesbian looking for love. 20–40

> *Here, Maddie explains why she prefers to look for that special someone in a bar rather than at more conservative venues.*

> *(Maddie, very femme, on a bar stool. She is dressed, if not to kill, at least to maim. To an unseen companion.)*

MADDIE: ...So I say to her, Rina, spare me the lecture. If you think it's sooo easy, meeting people in places other than bars, I am all ears! But you can skip the usual suspects.

Because I have been down the list, girlfriend, I have tried the recommended places, many times, but they just don't seem to produce. Cafes on certain nights. At the cafe bookstore, for example, if you make a precise looping maneuver between the Ani di Franco CD's and the Naiad mystery shelf, you can sometimes almost make eye contact with someone. As long as you don't stop too close to the Andrea Dworkin tracts. And people tell me that when a certain silky haired folksinger in torn jeans plays there, the picking up is very good, but I almost always get the dates mixed up and it's some macho dude poet making rhymed couplets about carburetors. Not that I have anything AGAINST carburetors or fan belts, especially when they're being replaced by some hunky Queen Latifah look-alike in coveralls, but I draw the line at bad slam poetry. No, the cafe bookstore is out. And their mocha latté, puhlease, if I'm going to pay four dollars and eighty-two cents for a beverage it had better have more in it than whipped cream! *(She raises her glass, toasts her companion.)*

Then Rina goes, why don't you go to the Center, I never see you there, it's a womyn-friendly alcohol-free space.

Oh, peachy, I say, that's a real upper, it's nothing but wall-to-wall support groups. Who wants to hear your own problems reflected back at you times ten. No it's not, she says, there are social events, too, and I say, get real! Country line dancing, no THANK you, it's like bad aerobics with hay stuck in your teeth, even the Chlamydia Support Circle looks good next to that. All those groups, they're as demoralizing as therapy, only without the relief or the attention.

Although I did fall for a really cute therapist once, big big blue eyes so full of sympathy, every time I looked into them I burst out crying, and that was hardly becoming. You just don't look your best when you're snuffling into your Kleenex. And it's extremely irritating to have to PAY to see someone you have a crush on, especially when there's an insurance deductible, and Blue Cross doesn't cover it anymore anyway.

At least in a bar you get pretzels with your longing.

Well, then why don't you volunteer somewhere, she says, and I say where? and she says, the Shelter always needs support. The Shelter?? Oh, now there's a prime place for picking up dates, all you see is women fleeing from one horror show or another. They're so desperate for a little kindness, it's like shaking down orphans, I just can't take the bottomless neediness.

Well how about Pride, she says, Daphne met her partner at a Pride organizing meeting, and okay—I admit that worked out for Daphne and Sue, but I really cannot sit through meetings, I endure enough of them at work. People arguing interminably about ludicrous nothings and if you're not careful you look at your calendar and it's nothing but wall-to-wall meetings, and they're always dominated by people who are experts at making the simplest decisions into Byzantine conspiracies. All you end up with is paper cuts from mailings or at best a half-price T-shirt and it's never even in your color.

Well, okay, the last one I went to I almost snagged a date. There was this really cute thing, and we were making some very intense eye contact, when the committee chairperson was exhorting people for the seven hundredth time about proper flyer distribution, and I started to hyperventilate, and so did she, and we were holding back giggles and for a moment I thought we would bust out of there and actually meet for a drink like real human beings—but then she had to go to the bulk mail facility and I haven't seen her since.

And then Rina goes: I think you are in denial, Maddie. About how ambivalent you are about your own community. If you spent more energy giving of yourself to the community, feeling EMPOWERED within your own community, you might actually be able to attract somebody decent and stable, instead of another in a chain of barfly losers, and I say, whoa whoa WHOA the last decent and stable person YOU introduced me to wanted to sell me insurance, and Rina, I have been to so many meetings, and so many potluck suppers, they are coming out of my eyes. How many more fricking tofu pecan crunch casseroles do I have to eat and time clocks do I have to punch before I am considered EMPOWERED WITHIN MY COMMUNITY? It's a never-ending list of obligations, this so-called community, it's like a second job, and fine, call me shallow, but sometimes I'd rather flirt, drink, and dance.

And she just LOOKS at me—with this withering look—and pow, off she sails, in a great big ole huff. And I think, oh great, Maddie, now you've done it, you're the traitor du jour, your picture is probably already up on her web site, "Click here for the latest Turncoat Lipstick Lesbian."

But, I ask you—what is the big deal problem with bars? Okay, so people maybe get a little loose, but at least here you know people are LOOKING. I mean, except for the ones who aren't looking, the ones who are merely waiting for their girlfriends to arrive, who are merely indulging in a little flirting before she gets there Big As Life. But some of them are looking. I hope. I mean, there's at least a CHANCE somebody's looking. (A pause to watch someone walk by—she's obviously a stunner.) Like that. Girlfriend! Did you ever see anything as fine as that at one of

Rina's pseudo-political potlucks? I don't THINK so. Although the ripped fishnets are a little much, don't you think?

But see! There is hope in here. Even though you have to keep running out in the alley to breathe because of all the smoke—and I know, the bathroom is a trial by ordeal, every time I put in my eyedrops I have to elbow my way to the mirror to fix my mascara or I'll look like a lost woodland creature—but here—at least there are women you might get to dance with. Now and then. When the music isn't too deafening, but I do carry my earplugs and they do help.

(Music gets loud. She reaches into her purse, puts earplugs in. Louder, as music gets louder.)

MADDIE: And okay, it does get a little crazy in here—but at least you know, as you look around this big, loud, crowded room: These Are Lesbians. All of 'em! Not just a dining room's worth of precertified, politically vetted, decent stable Longterm Prospects—unh-unh—Just lesbians! Lots of 'em. Coming out of the walls here, getting ready to rock the house down—

(Music crashingly loud by now—starting to dance in her seat.)

MADDIE: a big ole bunch of Lesbians Who Want to Party!

The Resurrection Play

Gabriel Lanci

Scene: a meeting of a support group for parents of murdered children

Dramatic
Lelia: a woman trying to come to terms with her daughter's violent death. 30–50

> *Here, Lelia addresses the group and relates the grim tale of her child's death.*

LELIA: When Bonnie was about four, George bought her a puppy—a taffy-colored spaniel. She named him "Bip"—we never knew where she got that name. It was something she invented on her own.
> *(Behind Lelia on the wall, a color photo is projected of a four-year-old girl. It appears as a blur at first, but then as the scene goes on, it becomes sharp and clear.)*

LELIA: A few months after she got him, Bip was hit by a speeding car. Bonnie was heartbroken. We tried to help her understand. George buried the puppy under a cherry tree in the garden. Bonnie watched him and placed some flowers on the grave. She asked us where Bip was now. George told her he was dead; he had stopped living. "Will I see him again," she asked? "Probably not," George told her. "I'll miss him," she said. "I know you will," George said, "but remember, Bip had a very happy time living with you, and you made him very happy". *(Beat.)* I try to remember Bonnie that way now, being happy with us. *(Beat.)*
> *(The photo has blurred and now fades out.)*

LELIA: One evening, two years ago, Bonnie didn't come home. We thought she might be at school, late, or with her friends somewhere. She always told us when she would be late, or phoned us if she became involved in something longer than usual. But we heard nothing. After a few hours we called her friends. They hadn't seen her. That was strange, because someone always saw Bonnie if you asked around. George finally called the police. They had us wait two days before we could declare her missing. Two days passed. The police began to search and found nothing. The days began to add up to a month. George and I went through the torment of not wanting to give up hope, and then not wanting to hope at all, that Bonnie was alive somewhere. She might have been injured, wandering, lost—we made up all kinds of stories to keep our sanity. *(Anguished.)* Bonnie had to be alive, we were so certain! Our friends said so…people prayed for us. *(Beat. Grim, darker voice.)* Then someone found something. *(Beat.)* It was miles away in some secluded woods somewhere in the mountains. They brought it in to the local police station and asked us to come there and look at it.

[MR. MARSHALL: *(From the audience.)* I don't want to hear this!]
[MRS. DONOVAN: *(From the audience.)* Then shut up so other people can!]

LELIA: They didn't have a morgue, just the sheriff's office…we had to go there. It was a building on the main street of the town. They brought us into an office, there was a large table in the center of the room and on the table something covered with a rubber sheet.

(On the wall behind her, a color photo is projected of the table with the covered form on it. It appears small at first and then slowly becomes larger until it fills the entire wall.)

LELIA: They asked George to look at it. He made me stand back so that I couldn't see when they lifted the sheet. I prayed it was not what we feared. *(Beat.)* I had forgotten what Bonnie was wearing that day she disappeared. I couldn't remember anything like that when the police had questioned me. When they lifted the sheet…a blue plaid fabric…I remembered…George was staring down. Then he turned to me and his face was like stone. He didn't say anything. I knew our friends were wrong, all the prayers had failed. Hope was now useless. *(Beat.)* I didn't get to see her. At the trial I did have to look at photographs of her. The face…had been eaten away by animals, only half of her scalp and some hair were left. Most of the open wounds on the body had rotted the flesh…the bone of the skeleton was visible. Her inner organs had either rotted or been eaten. It was a horror to look at! Something that had come out of my womb—. Something George and I had given life— We had held it close to us— Now *(Beat.)* it was gone, taken away. Not only destroyed, but made into putrid, rotting filth!

The Resurrection Play

Gabriel Lanci

Scene: a meeting of a support group for parents of murdered children

Dramatic
Mrs. Donovan: a woman whose spirit has been destroyed by her child's murder. 30–50

> *Here, a survivor angrily demands that the other members of the group always remember who the real victims of violent crime are: the children and their families.*

MRS. DONOVAN: Yes, go on with your lives. Forgiving, but forgetting who the victim is. The victim is not your daughter but you. Not our children, but us. And if you're the victim, justice is not your reward. You have to make it yours. You do that by force—by power—hatred. *(Turning to the audience.)* Yes! It's a good word! Learn it—hatred. Bobby's killer would be walking the streets today—probably with a few more strangled children to his credit. I let the law know who the victim was, because she was alive and screaming. They could not deny me. They convicted and sentenced him. That wasn't enough. I demanded to see him die. It was my right, my privilege, my justice. They could not deny me that. I was in the execution chamber when they brought him in. I watched them strap him into the chair. When they pulled the switch there was no sound, no movement except the creaking of the leather straps that held him against the current. *(Exultant.)* It was beautiful! *(To the audience.)* If that shocks you, learn the bitter truth—hatred, there is no sweet justice for you without it. *(Turning to Lelia.)* Christ you mock us! And you've turned your daughter's memory to shit!

A Seed Was Planted

Laurie Keith and Jeff Tabnick

Scene: a village in the Himalayas

Dramatic
Samantha: a young journalist facing a huge disappointment. 20s

> *Samantha has traveled to the remote Himalayas to observe a rare ritual that no westerner has ever seen. When she misses it by one day, she has a "postal" experience with the man who brought her to the village.*

SAMANTHA: I'm not going to be able to write my article now… Do you know why? Because I have nothing to write it on! I'm gonna return to New York, a journalist without a story. All those dreams I had of being the first person to write about this ritual are in the toilet.

    [*(He turns away.)*]

SAMANTHA: Hello? Do you know what it took for me to get here? Do you have any idea what I sacrificed? All day I worked in some boring magazine office and at night I busted my butt waitressing to drunks and perverts! I worked eighty hours a week. Do you know what that does to a person? Of course you don't, all you do is meditate in the woods and pick flowers. I lost friends, didn't get to see my family, I felt drained and exhausted all the time. But I wanted this, so I was willing to work for it. And what did I get? I'll tell you what I got—an intestinal disease! Do you know, I've had diarrhea for a week? And in this third-world hellhole, you call home, I can't even sit on a toilet to have my diarrhea. I have to squat over a big hole filled with shit and maggots! I have had nightmares about falling into that hole. My three biggest fears in life are death, getting pregnant, and falling into that shit hole! I haven't showered in a week, I'm sore, the altitude's makin' me feel like I'm on a bad acid trip! My hands and feet tingle! I'm hungry, but all there is to eat is candy bars from 1989 and soda that lost it's carbonation before I was even born! *(Beat.)* And it's not like I was trying to peak Mount Everest. For God's sake I was just trying to get to some dinky little village… What a waste… Do you think you could at least lead me to the airport? Could you at least do that for me?

> [*(He doesn't respond.)*]

SAMANTHA: Huh, mountain man?

> [*(He doesn't respond.)*]

SAMANTHA: What's the matter? All out of wise words?

Sensual Intelligence

Michael Farkash

Scene: here and now

Serio-Comic
Sheila: an obsessive mother. 40–50

> *Here, fanciful Sheila entertains one of her son's co-workers with the fable of his birth.*

SHEILA: I wish Tommy's father were still here. He's the only one who could control him. Do you know how Tommy's father and I met? We met on an exotic island. Samoa. You know Samoa?

[SOL: Isn't that where they pick kings by their size?]

SHEILA: Yes it is. *(Giggles.)* When I was very young, and very beautiful, I grew tired of my life as a manicurist in Yermo, California. So I went on a cruise. But on the cruise there was great trouble. The captain, fearing for the safety of the voyage, had me put off the ship. Why? Because I was so beautiful that the male passengers and crew were fighting over me, and endangering the ship. *(Pause.)* After my little lifeboat landed on the shore of Samoa, I fought my way through the surf and crawled into the nearest shelter, a giant conch shell. When I woke up the next morning, I climbed out of the pink seashell. Where my clothes were, only the Great Spirit knows! The first soul I met was Tommy's father, a handsome, bronzed young man, with a smile like perfectly matched pearls. He was to become the new king of Samoa. Kings were selected by their size. And Tommy's father was the biggest. We would row together in an outrigger, around the island. *(Sheila turns on tape player. It's a South Seas musical chant.)* By the light of the moon, we jigged, we loved. The moon swelled as hugely as my pregnant belly. I gave birth to Tommy in the surf, as Samoan women do. In those days, he was like a young god.

Singing in the Wilderness

Gabriel Lanci

Scene: backstage at the Beacon Theater, Boston. May, 1909

Dramatic
Mary Garden: a fiery Scottish soprano. 27

> *Oscar Hammerstein has brought his opera company to Boston to perform his version of* Salome, *based on Oscar Wilde's play. The mayor of Boston, however, has declared the work to be obscene and closed it down. Here, the soprano who was to be Salome confronts one of her detractors.*

MARY: Did I tell you, Olive Fermstead was right about the head.

[HAMMERSTEIN: The crazy woman who sang Salome at the Metropolitan?]

MARY: She is not crazy. She has a magnificent voice, Oscar, you should hear her. Olive went to the City Morgue and asked to hold a severed head. And they let her have one.

[HAMMERSTEIN: My God!]

MARY: She told me, "Honey, no young girl is goin' to dance around carryin' a head. It weighs a ton." It does, Oscar.

[HAMMERSTEIN: Jesus! You went to the morgue too!]

MARY: I just talked to the coroner. They didn't have a severed head available so they let me hold a man's head that was still attached.

[HAMMERSTEIN: O Christ! Stop it Mary, you're frightening me.]

MARY: The weight was amazing, Oscar. You could never realize how heavy something like that is. Now I know what they mean by "dead weight."

[HAMMERSTEIN: What do you need something like that for?]

MARY: *(Crossing to downstage.)* I take it inside, the weight, the feel, the look and texture of it, so that I can bring it to her—when I become the character. I have to translate to her meaning, to her sight, to her feeling.

(Light goes down on Hammerstein, comes up on Mary downstage.)

MARY: *(Beat.)* Are you Billy Sunday? *(Beat.)* Well Reverend Sunday, I am the woman you are preaching against—Mary Garden. *(Beat.)* Of course I don't look like a scarlet woman. I am not and never have been. I think you have the character and the performer confused. You see, Reverend, when you create a role, you must work from the inside—not with paint or fabric, but the soul of the character, the spirit. You can understand that, can't you. I thought a long time about that young girl, Salome, where she came from and where she went. Strauss says she went insane. I don't think Oscar Wilde would have agreed, but Strauss put it in the music. It begins at the end of the dance, where the tonality splits into discordant sound. At that moment I have her stand and look about at the veils she has strewn across the palace terrace. She sees her life lying there in pieces. But, she is young and the tragedy of being young—you must know this Reverend—is that you believe without doubt that you can never die. In the vicious mind death can become nonexistent, so that the death of others is without meaning. "I would have brought to me the head of Jokananhan on a silver tray," she says. Her stepfather thinks this is a childish prank. But this vicious girl is serious. She screams, "Give me the head of Jokananhan, now!" They give her what she asks for, she is so demanding. *(Beat.)* No Reverend, I don't think they spanked Judean princesses. With this terrible trophy comes unreason, insanity. It happens in a musical phrase, almost too sweet, too pure, that suddenly cracks open into horrifying dissonance, like a yawning pit, like a devouring beast. And so horrified are the watchers of this they destroy her completely. *(Beat.)* Where does she go, Reverend Sunday, where? Can she be forgiven in that place, is there such a forgiveness? *(Beat.)* I try to save her, but her fate is outside of my being, I cannot do it. Each night I bring her there to the yawning pit, to the edge of destruction. She goes gleefully, without thought of where she is headed. I want to cry out, "Wait! Think of what you are doing!" But words do not come to me, I am not myself, I am singing in a wilderness, I have given my body and my voice to her, and all I can do is follow. *(Beat.)* And then the moment comes when I must leave her, when the shields of the king's soldiers come crashing down upon her. She does not even scream. I cannot save her. *(Beat.)* Could you, Reverend Sunday? *(Beat.)* You think there is hope? I would not put it past me to hope. *(Beat.)* You know, on my way here, I noticed on the corner a drugstore with a soda fountain. Perhaps we might go there and have a soda. Yes, I will be glad to call you Billy, Reverend, if you will call me Mary, please. You know, they have nothing like ice cream sodas in France. The French would think of them as frivolous, if you can imagine such a thing.

Something Is Wrong

Robert Vivian

Scene: the deck of a house overlooking a vast lake

Dramatic
Louise: a middle-aged woman who feels she's missing an essential part of life. 52

> *While relaxing with her brother at the lake house, Louise reveals her sense of loss for something she can't even name.*

LOUISE: My wrist has a hollow place right here. Do you know what that means? Do you know what that augurs?

[LOUIS: No.]

LOUISE: You're fifty-five, I'm fifty-two. We're both healthy. But something is missing. Some tiny, little detail I can't get hold of. Maybe it should fit here in the hollow of my wrist. I don't know. I don't know. I can imagine its presence, feel its very slight weight, and yet I have no more hope of catching it than a rare butterfly. I think you know what I mean. The hardest part is knowing that you're damaged from birth. You're born without that vital part! You're lost without it, can hardly move without it. But somehow you manage. Somehow you sacrifice your whole life to something—you don't even know what it is—and after a while the routine becomes a kind of bandage. That must be why I'm a nurse. I'm in relatively good health and wear orthopedic shoes. I don't mind the sight of human shit. I understand the sight of blood because it's all we have, and patients send me flowers for looking after them. Send *me* flowers. *(Silence.)* Of course, all of it could come crashing down on my head the minute I get comfortable. That's the problem.

Something Is Wrong

Robert Vivian

Scene: the deck of a house overlooking a vast lake

Dramatic
Louise: a middle-aged woman who feels she's missing an essential part of life. 52

> *Happiness is something that can never exist in Louise's world as she here explains.*

LOUISE: I guess. Do you ever want to be alone?

[ELAINE JOY: No.]

LOUISE: Is it the one thing you fear more than anything in the world? I picture hell as a vast empty house where you can't make out the faces in the picture frames. Rain falls all day. You go from one room to another. One room to another. The only sound your dull footsteps in the hallway. Then at night...at night... What in God's name will you do?

[ELAINE JOY: If it's hell, you get on a stationary bike and try to fit into a size two.]

LOUISE: I don't want to be this way. But people who die in hospitals are always facing the light. What's wrong with them that they can't die in darkness? They don't want to be alone. They don't want to be like me and marry a man who's addicted to his own voice. But they can't help it. It beats being alone. I've held their hands, I've watched them fade away. You cannot tell me they wanted just a nurse to be there, just one nurse. Christ! I don't even know them! Where are there families, their loved ones, their pets and sons and daughters? Shouldn't there be a law against it? Who are we trying to fool? Something is wrong. Something I can't quite make out. I don't have the equipment to understand. But I don't believe in happiness. Not even a flicker. Jokes and vacations like this are something else, but happiness you may as well pour right down the drain. Because it doesn't exist. Not in a hospital, not in a cocktail, not on this deck.

Something Is Wrong

Robert Vivian

Scene: the deck of a house overlooking a vast lake

Serio-Comic
Elaine Joy: a woman struggling to maintain her marriage to an older man. 20s

> *Elaine's husband feels alienated by her energy. Here she speaks with wisdom past her age of her affection for him.*

ELAINE JOY: I've dated a lot of men. But it doesn't add up to much.
[LOUIS: Sex with you used to be a contest: I wanted to see if I could keep up with you. I always could. Now you're getting away from me.]

ELAINE JOY: I mention the other men because I'm not who I thought I was. I'm not who they want me to be. When you're younger you're capable of being twisted and pulled into all kinds of shapes, especially if you're desperate to please. I'm not so young anymore. When I married you I think I said to myself, This has to stop. The buck stops here. Because you can go headlong into a spiral with no bearing or reason on why you came here in the first place. I'm not who I thought I was. I was just a girl with fancy lipstick and tanned legs. But that only gets you so far. In fact, it has led up to this precise moment. *(Silence.)* I know why you married me. I know why we went to Cancun on our honeymoon. It was all part of a package deal we both bought into. But what we have now is not a package—unless it's one that's unraveling. Truth is, I like you a lot. I get a kick out of your morbid reflections. Your way of taking your first sip of coffee while staring out the window. The scrupulous way you clip your toenails over a trash can. The way you use the handsweeper to get every last one. You're very middle class in your habits. Lives are lost and won in just this way, you know. With caring and not caring how we look. It's the freedom to be godlike or a pig.

Stonewall Jackson's House

Jonathan Reynolds

Scene: a theatre lab

Dramatic
Tracy: an actress and playwright, African-American. 20–30

> *Tracy's new play has sparked raw discussion of racism among the members of her group. Here, Tracy speaks out with anger about the many misperceptions whites perpetrate through misguided efforts at political correctness.*

TRACY: Since I've known you. I'm such a different person from who you think I am. You don't have a clue what's on my mind, and you never will, 'cause most every time I see you, I lie. Most black people do. We say what we think you expect; and every time one of us tries to break through and act like an individual, clang, you close the jail bars on us.

> [JOE: All they've tried to do with their whole lives is make up for everything done to you for the last three or four centuries.]

TRACY: Well, please get them to *stop*. White people believe two things about race: one, that all people are created equal, and two, that blacks are inferior to whites. And now our massa-pleasing demagogues and your dilettante press have sprung to your aid, focusing on stupid distractions like reparations and was Beethoven black, theories about melanin dumb as phlogiston. I don't want reparations for some injustice done three hundred years ago! What if everybody demanded that? How far back should the blame go? Christians and lions? Ostrogoths and Vandals in 330 B.C.? "I'm an Ostrogoth, and I demand reparations for—"

The Sweat of My Brow

Daniel Kinch

Scene: here and now

Serio-Comic
Becky: an office worker. 20s

> *Here, hardworking Becky shares a poignant memory of her mother.*

BECKY: Oh, yeah. I got a tattoo. When you've just broken up with a boyfriend, you get a tattoo. With your food money. Two weeks before you graduate from college. Because you want to get a good job when you leave. Boy, did I hear about that. My parents always treated me like a screw-up. And when I went away to college, they still treated me that way. And in a way, they were right. 'Cause I'd do things like this. Not that I was a bad person, but I didn't like much playing by the rules, okay?

So I graduate...I think. I didn't get my diploma because I still owed the library fifty-three dollars in late fees, but I'm pretty sure I graduated. And I came home. And the bellyaching starts five minutes after I'm home. "You'll never get a job, you aren't responsible, who'd wanna hire you with that THING on your arm?." You know—encouragement. Mom and Dad did everything but try to get me into rehab. Mom especially was being her usual, dark self.

But I fooled mom. And myself. The day after I came home, I got a call from a friend of a friend that this law firm needed filing clerks. I could handle it. I showed up in a clean dress, they hired me. I was working three days after I moved home. Okay, the money was embarrassing even back then, but I had a JOB. I was correcting filings for this law firm that did really stupid stuff for rich people. They had rich clients who sued when their dishes broke during a dinner party. They had divorce cases that were too embarrassing for Sally Jesse to cover. I read about my firm in Cindy Adams, of all things. But it was a JOB. Mom couldn't harass me because I had a JOB.

And then, three months later, it was Christmas. And I'd been there just long enough to qualify for a bonus. And there is was—a check for four hundred and six dollars and thirty cents. It was so cool. I sat up til Mom came home from the night shift at the hospital and I showed her the check. I said, "Look mom. Here's my Christmas Bonus!"

And there was this awful silence as she looked at the check. And I thought, "Oh, great. She's gonna compare it to what my older brother makes at Con Ed. She's gonna compare me to my big sister, the NYNEX V.P. Or she's gonna compare it to her salary—she's a registered nurse in an I.C.U. unit. She saves lives. She's got lots of training." And my mother makes that sort of snorting laugh sound she makes when she's about to kick me in the teeth emotionally. And she says, "You wanna see MY Christmas Bonus?" What was I supposed to say? No?

So Mom reaches into her purse and she pulls out...a green pencil. It has "SouthSide Hospital Center"—the name of her hospital—stenciled on in yellow. And there's some slogan, like "Patient care is primary care," or something. Twenty-five years at the hospital, for five days a week and that's her bonus. And she laughed, sort of. She made this sad laughing noise and she said "Like it?" And I had to laugh too.

And I felt bad after that. Don't get me wrong—the attorneys at my place are crazy. I got a nasty memo once because I sent a client an e-mail and didn't put a capital G in the middle of his name—the attorney didn't know e-mail address wasn't case-sensitive. So I put up with crap. Everybody who works puts up with crap. But Mom saved lives. She would come home some nights with blood and vomit on her shoes from where some patient had been worked on. And the hospital had all these stupid rules—the hospital didn't pay overtime unless you stopped what you were doing and got a supervisor to sign off. So what?

Mom's supposed to stop giving cardiac massage just so she'd have a supervisor's John Hancock on her punch card?

And Mom knew her job was important—more important than me sorting papers for overpaid lawyers. She'd worked there twenty-five years and put her five kids through school with this job. But even though it was important, it wasn't important enough for someone to pay her decently for doing it. And it wasn't important enough for them to give her a bonus for coming in all those nights and making sure sick people were still alive the next morning when the doctors checked in.

Swing Lab

Steven Tanenbaum

Scene: N.Y.C.

Serio-Comic
DJ: a young Manhattanite in love with music and a teller of tales.
20s–30s

> *New York can be a hard town to make friends in as DJ's story
> illustrates.*

DJ: Three and a half city blocks may not seem like a great distance;
but when you multiply that number times 183, the new total
takes on a significance that you could never have calculated in
advance. You see, it's like this. Every morning, after my dog,
Irving, does his thing on the hydrant in front my building, I go to
get a get a cup of coffee at Cosmo's diner, which is half a block
from my apartment; but I never take the direct route. Instead, I
purposely walk in the wrong direction and needlessly circle the
block. The long way became necessary after I bought a *Times*
from the guy who owns the newsstand between my apartment
and the diner on the corner. I never purchased another thing
from him again—not a paper; not a Lotto ticket; not even a box
of Chicklets—but that didn't stop the man from doing the most
despicable thing. Every day after that first time, when I'd pass his
stand, he'd say, "Good morning." The nerve—I mean, every day
for six months, he said, "Good morning" to me; which was
undeniable proof that the man was one sick twist or worse, a
nice guy. My luck, turns out, he was a nice guy—had to be—
because after six months, it couldn't have just been a sales tactic.
And it definitely wasn't like he was hitting on me, either. You'd
know what I mean if you could see me from the waist down.
Trust me, that was the last thing on his mind. He was just being
nice which made it a hundred times worse; because eventually

the pressure of having to respond got so bad—after all, who could be expected to say, "Good morning" for six months straight. I mean, that's 183 days. So, I started to practice my delivery in my head as I approached his stand. "Good morning, Mr. Singh." No. "Hey Singh baby, what's happening." No, can't pull that off either. So, forget words—how about the cool nod thing. Yeah, just give him a nod of the head. On the approach, I practiced the nod; and kept practicing it over and over again until I had it down cold. The only problem was by the time I reached his stand, I had rehearsed it so many times I had drained the gesture of all it's spontaneity. Take it from me, if you try the cool nod thing when you're uptight, it ends up looking more like a spastic twitch than a greeting. I mean, I'm sure he thought it was one of my symptoms—you could see it in his eyes. So, fuck it; just take the long way around. Problem solved. Wrong. The whole time I was taking the long way around, I'd think, "I am so pathetic that I will walk three and half blocks out of my way everyday just so I don't have to say, 'Good morning, Mr. Singh.'"

(Cross fades to Ernest Ranglin's surfin'.)

DJ: Then, one morning, my brain decides to ratchet up the torment a couple of notches by looping that pathetic mantra so I could experience the shame on a nonstop basis. It was so annoying that I had to keep walking until it stopped. I walked right out of my neighborhood, past the Flat Iron Building, past Union Square, past the New School. When I got to West Fourth, I stopped. I don't know if it was the shouts or the heavy cloud of ganga or the rhythm coming from the boom box on the court; but the "Cage" had successfully distracted me. Without thinking, I automatically took a deserted spot by the chain-link fence, next to some German tourists, and watched the current crop of playground legends shoot the rock. I stood there for fifteen minutes which is exactly how long the voice inside my head remained quiet. I mean, what I was watching was undeniably impressive. There was this group of people; and they were doing the typical things that people do—you know, shout, push, sweat, curse: Normal stuff; but with one major exception, they were also enjoying every second of it. That kind of circumstance is so rare even the neurotic voice inside my head had to stop talking and take notice. Then, at the very same moment, both voices—neurotic and rational—had the exact same response: "Hey, I wanna do that." I don't mean play basketball. I mean, have fun. But in order to have fun you have to do something you enjoy. Yeah, what do you enjoy…

(Cross fades to blues walk.)

DJ: …The hip hop cut coming out of the boom box slowly coaxed an incomplete association from the past that would not cohere until I recognized the sampled beat under the rapper's words. It was one of those infectious, swinging beats that I first heard played by the man who made me pray every night that my own father would die in his sleep so he could adopt me. And for the first time that day I smiled. Only problem was that the German tourist standing next to me thought it was meant for him. He pointed to the court and said, "Good ball." I closed my eyes and nodded to the music…

Swing Lab

Steven Tanenbaum

Scene: N.Y.C.

Serio-Comic
DJ: a young Manhattanite in love with music and a teller of tales.
20s–30s

Here, philosophical DJ tells the tale of a love affair gone bad.

DJ: Now, I can confidently say that the seamier side no longer holds me in its thrall. Or, to put it another way, I used to think that when the right kind of guy was a little dirty around the edges— you know—had the requisite amount of greasy hair and grime on his clothes—the whole scruffy bit—that it signified danger. Now I think the only thing a guy like that should get intimate with is a *loofah.* My last boyfriend had the seamy and vamp thing down pat. In retrospect the aspect that I find most amusing about his look was that it was a choice. At some point, he actually decided that dirty was the way to go. I mean, it couldn't have been an accident if the guy had a framed picture of Herbert Hunke on his wall.

(*Cross fade to Willie Bobo's black coffee.*)

DJ: You know, the Times Square hustler who all the Beats thought was the purest and realest soul. Well, at least my boyfriend paid lip service to his historical precedent. Most downtown types who use squalor to accessorize don't have a clue that they're aping a guy, who in all likelihood, would've pegged 'em for a square and boosted their wallet the first chance he got. Now, if I encountered a guy with a framed picture of Herbert Hunke on his wall it would only signify one thing to me: wiping is not an obsession. But, by the time I was hip to that, it was too late. You see, the man had the most eclectic assortment of head bobbin' music in his record collection—everything from T-Bone Walker to Willie Bobo. I mean, you gotta be impressed that the same guy who listened to *You're Wanted by the Police and My Wife Thinks You're Dead* was also hip to *The Inflated Tear*. You see, as far as I'm concerned, a record collection is the best character reference. Provided of course, that the records aren't stolen property. See, if I had known that up front, I would have made a citizen's arrest on the spot; because for me, stealing music is a capital crime. But you have a tendency to overlook even the most obvious clues when you're the victim of a felonious seduction. My boyfriend could look me straight in the eye and tell me with the utmost sincerity every lie I ever wanted to hear. The man was a master of finesse; I mean, not once did I ever see him turn off my bullshit detector. The fact that he never stopped refreshing my drink the whole time definitely helped. I think when I'd enter that vulnerable state between passed out and blacked out, he must've made subliminal suggestions—I mean, what else can explain my behavior. You know, first it starts out with fronting a couple of bucks until payday—which he conveniently forgets to repay because he never had a job in the first place. After that occurs again at the most strategically executed interval, he's ready to make the big move. Of course, not before he bats his eyes and demonstrates his only marketable skill which is guaranteed to separate a female fool from her money even before the last toe has uncurled. Only then, when the postcoital high has kicked in, does he hit you up for his rent—which he can't cover this month because he had to help out an old friend who was down on his luck. Translated, that means if he doesn't come up with the money his good buddy the loan shark will break his knee caps. I don't know why it was so hard to see through him.

(Cross fade to T-Bone Walker's feeling the blues.)

DJ: Even at this late date, I'm not sure I can pinpoint what was the drug and what was the trip. I mean, was alcohol the drug that made sex possible or was sex the drug that made staying tolerable. In either case, you definitely can't eliminate sex from the mix. As you can tell, I didn't get out unscathed. But at least I got custody of the dog. He had this great dog: a really good-natured

mutt that looked like a black bear cub. We belonged together—
me and that mutt—because we had both swallowed more than
our fill. But back to that last night. We had gone to see 'Spoon
at the blues club on 14th and I had brought along an album for
him to autograph. I don't know if 'Spoon is sixty or a hundred
because as you watch him struggle to the stage on crutches in a
torturously slow manner, your heart starts to sink; but as soon as
the waitress puts a snifter of his favorite libation under his chair
and he counts off the beat, the years start to melt away, one by
one, as he belts the blues.

After the last set, I shyly approached 'Spoon and he gra-
ciously signed my album cover. We hadn't gone more than two
steps when my boyfriend said it. To me, it was undeniable proof
that the man was the worst kind of faker and that he couldn't be
the rightful owner of the records in his collection. In earshot of
'Spoon, my boyfriend said, "It's a good thing you got his autograph tonight because he looks like he's gonna croak any second." I didn't turn around because I was sure that 'Spoon had
heard him; and if anyone was going to die at that moment, it was
going to be me. During the ride home in the cab, I had to keep
reminding myself that I was pissed and to lift my head off his
shoulder everytime I nodded out. But I was too ginned up to
maintain my resolve and the next thing I can remember is lying
on my back on the kitchen table with my ankles over my head as
he managed to demonstrate some semblance of carnal knowledge. When he was on automatic like that, nothing could distract
him. Not the alcohol; not the dog who was going nuts the whole
time; not even the reality that he was only screwing a mark. At
that point, all I could think was what a time to sober up. The
room reeked of booze and stale smoke; and everytime the
kitchen table shook, I was sure that I was going to puke all over
the place mats.

Finally, finally, he grunted and pulled out. When I lifted my
head and the blurred vision eased up enough for me to see, I
espied him shuffling out of the room with his pants around his
ankles. Then, I was distracted by a slurping sound. His dog was

130

underneath the table lapping up his sperm from the floor... Don't you just love it when life paints you a picture. Needless to say, it was at that precise moment that I decided it was over...and that I would keep the dog. You see, this is where the line about both of us having swallowed our fill comes into play. The next morning I told him; and when I came home from work, he was gone. And so were a few other items. My television, my VCR, and most crushing of all, my record collection. The bastard cleaned me out—I called the police but what could they do, put Thelonious Monk's picture on a milk carton. Well, at least I came out of it with the mutt, who I immediately rechristened, Irving, and something else that's very important...

(Turn down the volume.)

DJ: ...A new definition of true love. True love is being able to watch a dog lap up your man's cum from the floor and not for one second see that image as any kind of metaphor for your relationship.

Tidworth

Jocelyn Beard

Scene: a village on the Salisbury Plain, England, 1669

Dramatic
Dannyth Moore: a midwife; ancient and wise. 50–80

> *The wife of the local magistrate, Anna Mompresson has come to Dannyth for help regarding unusual disturbances in the Mompresson home. Here, the canny midwife muses on Anna's strange situation.*

DANNYTH: One, two, three, four five, six, seven, eight, nine. The Reverend Boswell's bitch heaved out nine pups under a waxing moon. He counts them in the whelping box. One, two, three, four, five, six, seven, eight, nine. Night and day. He counts them. His servants count them. His Majesty's census taker has counted them. Every child in Tidworth can number the litter. One, two, three, four, five, six, seven, eight, nine. Only the bitch doesn't count them. She knows them not by their number but by their smell. By the sting on her nipples as they suckle her. She knows them by the beating of their hearts. Each rhythm unique under the stars. One, two, three, four, five, six, seven, eight, nine. *(Pause.)* Anna Wesslyn's was as difficult a birth as I am able to recall. So twisted was she in the womb that I feared for hours to lose them both. But she untwisted. She found her way out into the world. One. One child for Robert and Jane Wesslyn. One. One child for Harold and Elizabeth Mompresson. One. One added to one made for…more than one. *(Pause.)* When Anna came to find me that day I knew in my bones that we were all in for a time. Her cheeks were as red as I've ever seen 'em. Her eyes glittered with the same stuff that got her untwisted and out into the world. That stuff is potent. It's the most potent stuff in life for it fuels all endeavor. Without it, we're just counting pups. One, two, three, for, five, six, seven, eight, nine.

Tikkun Olam: Repairing The World

Paula J. Caplan

Scene: a high school awards banquet

Dramatic
Mag: a woman reunited with old high school friends. 50s

A school function has brought old friends together again. As they trade memories and updates, each reveals something of the past that has haunted them. Here, Mag speaks with poignance of her relationship with her mother.

MAG: I can't imagine how it must have felt to have a loving mother. When I was a senior at Greenwood, a neighbor brought her new baby over, and Mom held that baby and smiled at it. And I was shocked…because she never touched me, and whenever I touched her, she'd always say, "Keep your clammy hands off me!"

[JULIA: *(Emphatically.)* How awful.]

MAG: Well, my palms were always sweaty.

[ROSIE: Why was she so mean?]

MAG: I've never been sure. I know her father was very stern and died when she was young. Mom had to give him back rubs, and they had to last sixty minutes, never fifty-nine. He made her polish all the wood in their huge mansion and used a hairbrush on her when he got mad. My dad was just as stern and even older than her father. When they got married, she only weighed ninety pounds, and hardly gained anything while she was pregnant. When I was born, it took me four months to get to weigh six and a half pounds. Mom was always going to a tuberculosis sanitarium nearby, and I remember her showing me needle marks on her arms from her "treatments." But it was odd…no one ever even tried to say she had T.B.

'Til the Rapture Comes

Edward Napier

Scene: post WWII West Virginia

Dramatic
Althea: a veteran of WWII and recovering barbiturate addict

> *Following her experiences as a nurse in the war, Althea allowed herself to become addicted to prescription medication and bad behavior. Now home and trying to get it together, she is confronted by her Pentecostal housekeeper with the fact that there are many in town who know about her less wholesome activities. Here, Althea explodes with anger and indignation.*

ALTHEA: What did you do? During the War? Clean house? Work for Armco Steel over in Kentucky? You cheap son-of-a-bitch. You have no idea what it is to go to War. How it was. What I saw! Everybody so goddamn happy the War was over. Jubilation! When I had never known so much emptiness. Such despair. Because I knew that nobody had won this goddamn War. I knew it when I saw my Mother's face after my brother, Ian, died. I knew as I held young boy after young boy as they died in my arms, asking for their mothers like children. I knew when my girlfriends and I took leave while we were stationed in Berlin and went to see a death camp especially for women and children called Ravensbruck. And after we killed all those Japs in Nagasaki and Hiroshima with the atom bomb. I knew. This is the War that nobody is going to win. This is the War where the whole world went to hell. And I kept wondering, everywhere I went in England and Scotland and France and all over this country in the years immediately following the surrender of Jodl and Umezu, what in the hell are all of these son-of-a-bitches so happy about?

[PETUNIA: They were relieved the War was over, Althea. That's what they were.]

ALTHEA: The War wasn't over. It's still not over! And let me just tell you, Petunia Mae Thacker: I don't give a good goddamn what any of these people in town say about me. Or what they know.

Two Birds, One Stone

Caroline Rosenstone

Scene: here and now

Serio-Comic
Kathy: a high-strung sardonic woman confronting demons from the past. 30s

> *Kathy's strained relationships with her father and her husband had a strange convergence as she here relates.*

KATHY: Today's my father's birthday, so even though I'm out of a job, I ran right out to buy myself a present. *(She points to her necklace.)* Like an old piece of shoe leather, he won't wear out. I hear from my source—my cousin Patrice—that now he's taken to swimming everyday in his condo pool. Aerobic exercise! Patrice reports that his eyesight's failing, and he's had accidents. Tripped over the cord running to the fan stuck up on some kitchen shelf, and the fan fell on his head. (Still too goddamn cheap to use the air conditioner.) He was nicked on his bald pate but otherwise fine. Then he rode himself on his bicycle straight into a river. But the river wasn't sufficiently deep. *(She looks at the necklace.)* This is a river pearl!

Our sad jokes go way back. Years ago, when my sister Donna and I were still in deep denial, we sent him this mail-order chocolate cake for Easter. Chocolate cake, chocolate icing, chocolate chips: We didn't skimp. He wrote back, "You forgot I'm diabetic." "Yeah?" We said it in unison, like a vaudeville act: "Yeah?" *(She examines her necklace.)* Pretty, but no diamond. Diamond-*like*. Anytime a woman buys herself something like this, you know what's on her mind...the "he" word. HE wears a dopey spool of keys hanging from the belt loops of his Docker's pants, has this frizzy pouf of khaki hair, white-bread features like the kid on Andy of Mayberry—you could've knocked me over with a tube of spermicidal jelly I'd go for someone like him. Usually, take a man who's unemployable, just released from prison, more of a coke-head than Richard Pryor, so cynical he's a human source for battery acid; please God, make him homosexual—usually, take a man with a few of those qualifications, and honey, you're calling my name!

And his name? *Ed?* But one day Ed reaches across your desk, clicking on your mouse to call up some spreadsheet, and there arises in you this strange fondness for…his knuckles. You want to bend down over his hairy wrist and give those tender mounds a little lick. Invite him home for dinner and feed him hearty bean soups thick with vegetables, steamed artichokes…leaf by leaf…in bed…where we never ended up.

Which is just as well, because Ed was my boss, but a boy. A real *scout.* Dependable, gentle, trustworthy—like working for a golden retriever. Complete with the khaki hair, which falls over his forehead in neat clumps.

My immediate problem is that I'm out of a job. Ed fired me.

History lesson. Ed's father, Ed Sr., who founded Complete Security, was, like his son, a computer geek for whom designing foolproof burglar alarm systems for every client was the daylight equivalent of a wet dream. Fanatical, Ed Sr. committed to memory the four-digit security codes of all of his clients, engendering loyalty and statewide referrals. Lo, the business grew, as did Ed's good and upright son Ed. When Parkinson's disease carved a niche in the otherwise chock-full brain of the father, the son stepped in to captain the ship, man the mast…however the hell you want to talk about it. Okay?

When Ed—my Ed—Ed Jr. took over the business, he completed the Complete Security picture by adding our Home Health Alert system, which wired not only businesses and homes, but, if they so chose, the clients themselves to a monitored alarm. Clients wear a pendant around their necks; in the event of a personal emergency, they beep us and we send in the troops. It's a popular gift for the elderly living alone, handicapped people… *(Mockingly.)* "Help, I'm falling and I can't get up."

You've heard those commercials. That's the Lifephone people. No class. Our referrals are word of mouth. By adding the health area to the business, Ed killed two birds with one stone. His father, home alone with the Parkinson's, was the first person he hooked up to a pendant; plus, he put his own stamp on the business. For Ed, those were two good birds.

This guy beeps us—a personal emergency call. In like half a second I get to him on his intercom. He's in a wheelchair, just woke up from a nap to discover his cat's scratched its way into his catheter bag. He was nuts; I talked him down and had the medics there in three minutes. I told the guy, what if we call this a code yellow. He laughed. See, I understood. This wasn't a life-threatening emergency: it was worse.

Usually there's not much give-and-take in these calls. You're talking to someone who's just jammed an arterial vein in a hand down on a knife sticking up from the dish rack before they've even had their morning coffee. They give you the bad news, then whimper to themselves; or they scream at you like it's your fault you're on the phone and not standing next to them, winding them up in a tourniquet. So unless Lillian's out and I have to pinch-hit on the answering service, I take the low road and run the office. Handle accounts, every piece of correspondence, which I write, as in *compose*.

So—I showed up every day, fifteen minutes late but otherwise on good behavior. Pretty soon it was two years. Ed went with me to the dealership when I bought my used car so they'd see a man in the picture, not be so quick to screw me. To celebrate, he took me to a "nice" restaurant—tablecloth, carnation, salad bar with five choices of dressing—Ed loves bleu cheese— and gave me this good luck thing to hang from my rearview mirror. *(She takes a sequined bird in a cage from her purse and unwraps it.)* When his father died, I made him a casserole. The vegetables bright green, fresh, from a farmer's market way up north.

In that all the parts were there but I didn't hear anything ticking, the whole thing came down like a bomb. March 27. Lillian had a wedding shower for her daughter, so I took over the phones. Lillian's got this calendar of daily spiritual sayings on her desk. March 27 read "Pray to God, but tie your camel." Okay. Ed's out on the road. We start slow. A 910 came in—personal emergency; this old lady from out in West Hartford. She'd found a lizard swimming among the towels in her washing machine: called us because she didn't know what else to do.

I said, "Take one cup of Tide, two cups of Clorox, pour it over the lizard, and call me in the morning." Then I got hold of her son. "Mr. Lipman, I think I hear your mother calling you." *(She takes a printout of the alarm activations records from her purse.)* Typical stuff came in—a 562, a burglar alarm…false; a 781—fire alarm…real; then a 910—personal emergency…real…a heart case out in Simsbury.

2:25 P.M., another 910: medical emergency. "I hurt my head," the guy says. You know how you cannot hear a voice for a dozen years, and know right away who it is? Even in its old, sickly incarnation. "I hurt my head." I didn't say a word. My tongue cleaved to the roof of my mouth. I used his code to access his name. It's him. He's living in Easton. Lillian's calendar page reads, "Pray to God but tie your camel." What? I disconnect the call.

2:54 Easton. Louder. "I hurt my head." My heart is a gong pounding through my ears. "Hello? Can't you hear me? I hurt…" But I can't hear. I lean down, unstrap my shoes, let my feet breathe. Disconnect the call.

2.57 Easton. Some vibration on the line, but I can't make out the words. I'm writing on my report sheet, "Milky Way." When I was a little girl, we walked hand in hand down the street and named the constellations…

And then my older sister Donna got sick and needed steroids, which meant money, and Dad had to work a second shift. Cortisone made her blow up like a balloon. Dad came up with a secret sport. When Mom left for the store, he'd go in Donna's room, pick her up by one hand like a bowling ball, and throw her down the stairs. "You fucker," he'd yell. I'd follow her down the stairs, crying and useless. When Mom came back, he'd be sweet as pie. Had we been dreaming? Seeing things? And Donna ended up with double vision in her left eye, and a nose shaped like the back end of a spoon. Easton? I can't hear you, Easton. This obstruction on the line.

You could say, as Ed does, that I was in a position of responsibility, and I did nothing. Or you could say that I did...something. "Pray to God, but tie your camel." What does that mean? It means...take things into your own hands. If what goes around comes around, I just gave that wheel a little push.

My father's cleaning lady did her part. Found him six hours later, called the police, saved his life. His head bashed in by a bookcase that crashed down out of the blue—the hand of God?—he hung on, tenacious as a little rat. Ratlike, now he's after Ed, threatening to sue. This could go to court. The alarm activation records subpoenaed. As soon as my father came after Ed, I told Ed the whole thing, blow by blow, and why. I'll tell it all in court. In front of everyone. Big day. Ed looks at me like I'm his worst nightmare. Dirt.

How dare you. In your happy ignorance. Go on, Ed, live in your world the size of a thimble. Keep it small and clean. Sorry, baby: minus the damage to you, no regrets. I'd do it again. *(She touches the necklace.)* This cost me my last twenty bucks, but today...today I needed something pretty.

Two Nights Near Doolin

Louisa Burns-Bisogno

Scene: a pub in Ireland

Dramatic

Peg: a woman who has just been located by the son she gave up for adoption. 50s

> *Peg fell in love with an American photographer who disappeared without a good-bye. Pregnant, Peg allowed her sister, Maura to convince her to give the baby up for adoption. Years later, her son has tracked her down, prompting a long-silent family member to reveal that the photographer had been murdered and that Maura led the killers to him. Here, Peg lashes out with rage and grief at the sister who betrayed her.*

PEG: It was you did it!

(Peg throws herself at Maura…trying to choke her. They tumble down the few steps to the floor. As they struggle.)

[MAURA: Peg! Stop! It was an accident!]

PEG: It was murder! Murderer!

[*(Sean pulls Peg off Maura.)*]

[SEAN: God'll judge her!]

[MAURA: The Lord is my witness…I meant only to frighten the man. So he'd wash his hands of us as he'd washed his hands of the Troubles. Then, he'd go back to America. And leave us in peace as we were.]

PEG: There's never been peace between us. You always begrudged me. Our mother's affection. My gift of music. Sean's attachment. But mostly Matthew. And the life he offered me. *(To Sean.)* She didn't just bribe you, Sean. She bribed me, too. "I'll help cover up the pregnancy," she said. "None need ever know the sinful fool you've been." I had no money of my own, a sick old mother…so

I went to Dublin as Maura arranged. I signed the papers promisin' me baby for adoption. At night I lamented with the music. My baby must've heard it for he kicked and kicked when I sang. Remindin' me I had someone else to live for. And so I secretly planned a way out. I was writin' to our brother in the States…when my time came suddenly. They held me down. I never saw my son born. But I heard his sweet cry as they carried him away. "Don't look on him, not once"… Maura had warned me…"It'll break your heart and you'll regret it to your dyin' day." I didn't care about myself. Only for me baby. In pain and bleedin', after all the lights were out…I made my way to the Nursery. *(Peg picks up the fiddle from the floor and cradles it like a baby.)* The nurse caught me. When I wouldn't give him up to her, she sent for Maura. *(To Maura.)* "Hand him over!" you demanded. Then, one by one…you bent my fingers back saying…none would help me. That I'd destroy myself along with our family." Still I held onto my son. But you knew how to break my will…"Your bastard will starve with you. Is that what you want? Ye may as well kill him now and spare him a life of shame and sufferin'" *(Slowly her fingers release the violin, she lays it on the bar.)* Fear for me son overcame me. I let him be taken by Maura. Handed over to strangers! *(A beat.)* How can he forgive me?

Virtual Rendezvous

Michael Sepesy

Scene: here and now

Serio-Comic
She: an on-line chatter looking for cyber thrills. 20s

> *Here, a young married woman enjoys a virtual rendezvous
> with disappointing results.*

SHE: Night, sweetie.
> [*(He exits. She waits until he's gone, then practically pounces
> on the monitor.)*]

SHE: Now. Where are you? Venus Lounge…Lovers Chat Room…
oh God. He's there. He's there. Manuel9. *(Typing.)* "Hi, Hot Stuff.
Where were you last night?" *(Reads.)* "Thinking of you." Oh jeez.
Is this guy for real? *(Types.)* "Would you like to take another walk
through the streets of Paris?" Great. *(Types.)* "I've always wanted
to kiss under the Arc de Triomphe. Holding hands." *(Reads.)*
"Your eyes are magic." Well. My eyes are magic. Umm. *(Types.)*
"Let's play the violin and dance under the moon along the
Champs Élysées." *(Reading, then.)* Oh. You forgot to ask what I
look like. Fuck. *(Types.)* "Tall. Young. Blonde. Thin." What?
(Reads, giggles, types.) "Yes. They're real. Blushing." *(Reads.)* Ah.
You enjoyed our "trip" to the Italian Riviera. *(Types.)* "So did I."
(Reads.) Am I married? *(Looks behind her, then types.)* "No."
(Reads.) You like me a lot. *(Types.)* "I like you, too. We've never
even met but…Maybe it's the champagne." *(She holds up her
beer. Reads.)* You'd like to meet me sometime. I'd love to meet
you. *(Types.)* "I don't think that would be a good idea." *(Reads.)*
"Why not?" Yeah. Why not? *(Types.)* "There are risks. You hear
all those stories." *(Reads.)* "Love is an adventure." *(Types.)* "Stop
it or I really will fall in love." *(Reads.)* "I'm already there." *(Silence.
She stops. Looks back. Then at her computer. Drinks. Types.)*

"Where could we meet?" *(Silence, then types.)* "Hello?" *(Silence.)* Shit. Oh. There you are. *(Types.)* "I thought I scared you away." Wait. Go? *(Types.)* "What do you mean you have to go? The night is still young. Was it something I said?" *(Reads.)* "My mommy wants me to go to bed." *(Types.)* "How old are you?" *(Reads. Types.)* "No. I'm not mad at you. Good night, Manuel." *(She sits back. Drinks.)* Well. We'll always have Paris.

Wanda Dresses for the Evening

Bill McMahon

Scene: a bedroom

Serio-Comic
Wanda: a woman determined to enjoy an evening out—no matter what. 30–50

> *When a marital squabble turns deadly, Wanda decides not to waste an opportunity to get out of the house.*

WANDA: *(Picks up something else from table and flings it at him.)* I am not a piece of trash! *(Walks toward bed, stands over him menacingly.)* I don't mind being decorative, I don't mind your bouts of depression, I don't mind your head trips—well, I do, actually, but I can put up with them—BUT I WILL NOT HAVE YOU DISRESPECT ME.

[STEWART: *(Clutching head.)* Bitch!]

WANDA: *(Purposefully calming herself; Stewart continues to moan in pain.)* Whatever. I see myself as a professional, Stewart. I am a professional wife. I am here to help you keep up appearances, which I do excellently, if I say so myself. I enjoy my work, I put a lot of myself into it. Now anywhere else in the workforce, such an employee would command respect. I feel I'm entitled to it. But when you get all gooey and needy and messy, when you try to drag me into your personal icky little emotional life, well that's just not in the job description.

[STEWART: *(Grasping head with one hand, chest with other, short of breath.)* Don't…go…Wanda, I…oh, God…the pain—]

WANDA: *(Going to dresser, gets bottle of pills, hands him one.)* For God's sake, take the fucking pill!

[STEWART: Not…just my…head…Wanda! *(He falls backward onto bed, clutching chest.)*]

WANDA: Stewart, this is not—Stewart? *(She goes closer, looks at him.)* Oh, Jesus Christ, are you having a heart attack? Now?

   [*(Stewart is unable to speak.)*]

WANDA: Lord, gimme a break already! *(She gets on bed over him, begins to do CPR.)* Not now, Stewart, this is not a good time. *(Breathes into his mouth, pumps his chest.)* Breathe, damn it! *(Listens to his chest, breathes into mouth, pumps his chest.)* Come on, you dolt! *(Relentlessly repeating the CPR.)* I mean it, Stewart! I'm not letting you do this... *(No effect. She practically beats on his chest. He is totally morbid. She is exhausted.)* You're beyond 911, aren't you? *(She feels at his neck and wrist for a pulse.)* Oh, great. Anything to spoil my evening. You go to such extremes, Stewart. *(She sits at edge of bed, looks at him. A beat.)* You only want more because you know you can't have it. You wanted coldness from me, Stewart. I think my coldness kept you going. *(She rises from bed, walks to door, calls out.)* Roger! Roger, I need help here! *(She suddenly remembers.)* Roger's not here. We're alone. *(She looks at her watch.)* Seven thirty. More than sufficient. *(She goes to mirror, adjusts hair and make-up. She speaks to Stewart's body.)* After all, I'm sure the coroner won't be able to fix time of death any closer than within two hours, will he? *(She puts on dress. She is resplendent.)* I mean, there really is nothing else you'll be needing this evening, and I do deserve a night off, don't I? Sorry the dress isn't black, but it's not my best color, and I don't officially know you're dead yet, after all. Besides, I'd better start networking for my next gig. I know your relatives will all make a huge fuss about the will. *(She puts on wrap.)* "Her night of social brilliance ends in tragedy." Tomorrow's *Times*. And *News,* and *Post,* and *W.* The mystique of a widow, and sympathy to boot. Thanks, dear. For all your faults, you always did have a thoughtful side to you. *(She checks herself in mirror.)* I'm sorry you couldn't have been happier with the agreement, Stew. But it's best to stick to the letter of the contract. There isn't much room for going outside the lines. *(She goes to door.)* Good night, Stewart. Don't wait up.

Permissions Acknowledgments